TOUCHPOINTS BIBLE PROMISES

God's Answers for Your Daily Needs

TouchPoints

BIBLE PROMISES

GOD'S ANSWERS FOR
YOUR DAILY NEEDS

Tyndale House Publishers, Inc.
Wheaton, Illinois

Visit Tyndale's exciting Web site at www.tyndale.com

Scripture selection and note writing primarily by Douglas J. Rumford

General editors: Ronald A. Beers and V. Gilbert Beers

Contributing writers: Douglas J. Rumford, Rhonda K. O'Brien, V. Gilbert Beers, Ronald A. Beers, Shawn A. Harrison, Jonathan Gray, and Brian R. Coffey.

Tyndale House editor: Shawn A. Harrison

ISBN 0-8423-4227-3

Printed in the United States of America

07 06 05 04 03 02 01
10 9   8   7   6   5   4   3   2

PREFACE

Psalm 119:111, 162 *Your decrees are my treasure; they are truly my heart's delight. . . . I rejoice in your word like one who finds great treasure.*

Psalm 119:91, 160 *Your laws remain true today; for everything serves your plans. . . . All your words are true; all your just laws will stand forever.*

Psalm 119:105 *Your word is a lamp for my feet and a light for my path.*

What a treasure we have in God's word! The Holy Bible is relevant to today's issues and gives solid guidance for daily living.

In this book you will find over one hundred topics for daily living and what the Bible says about each one. Each topic is listed alphabetically and is accompanied by several questions, Scripture passages, and comments. In the index at the back of this book, you will find a complete listing of all the topics for quick reference. You can read through this book page by page or use it as a reference guide for topics of particular interest to you.

While we could not cover all topics, questions, and Scriptures related to the subject of this book, our prayer is that you will continue to deliberately search God's word. May you find God's answers as he longs to be your daily guide. Enjoy your treasure hunt!

THE EDITORS

2 Timothy 3:16-17 *All Scripture is inspired by God and is useful to teach us what is true and to make us realize what is wrong in our lives. It straightens us out and teaches us to do what is right. It is God's way of preparing us in every way, fully equipped for every good thing God wants us to do.*

ABANDONMENT

Will God abandon me during my hard times?

Psalm 27:10 *Even if my father and mother abandon me, the LORD will hold me close.*
Even if those on whom we most rely desert or neglect us, God never will. In fact, our difficulties can become the means to experience God's presence even more intimately.

Does God promise to be with me at some times, but not at others?

Matthew 28:18, 20 *Jesus came and told his disciples, . . . "Be sure of this: I am with you always, even to the end of the age."*

John 14:16 *I will ask the Father, and he will give you another Counselor, who will never leave you.*

2 Corinthians 4:9 *We are hunted down, but God never abandons us. We get knocked down, but we get up again and keep going.*

Hebrews 13:5 *Stay away from the love of money; be satisfied with what you have. For God has said, "I will never fail you. I will never forsake you."*
God promises to be present with us, in us, and beside us in all circumstances.

ABUNDANCE

see also Giving, Provision

Under what circumstances does God promise abundance to us?

Malachi 3:10-11 *"Bring all the tithes into the storehouse so there will be enough food in my Temple. If you do," says the LORD Almighty, "I will open the windows of heaven for you. I will pour out a blessing so great you won't have enough room to take it in! Try it! Let me prove it to you! Your crops will be abundant, for I will guard them from insects and disease. Your grapes will not shrivel before they are ripe," says the LORD Almighty.*

Philippians 4:19 *This same God who takes care of me will supply all your needs from his glorious riches, which have been given to us in Christ Jesus.*
God's abundant provision is a gracious gift. When we give what God requires we receive more than we could ever desire.

Deuteronomy 30:9 *The LORD your God will make you successful in everything you do. He will give you many children and numerous livestock, and your fields will produce abundant harvests, for the LORD will delight in being good to you as he was to your ancestors.* God is not stingy and resentful in supplying our needs. He loves to lavish his abundance on those with grateful hearts.

Why does God give us abundant gifts?

2 Corinthians 9:8 *God will generously provide all you need. Then you will always have everything you need and plenty left over to share with others.* God wants us to have everything we need. But we don't get to keep what we receive; we get to give it away. God is looking for us to share his abundance with others.

ABUSE

see Comfort, Suffering

ACCEPTANCE

see also Forgiveness, Grace

How can I know that God accepts me?

Romans 3:30 *There is only one God, and there is only one way of being accepted by him. He makes people right with himself only by faith, whether they are Jews or Gentiles.*

Galatians 2:16 *We Jewish Christians know that we become right with God, not by doing what the law commands, but by faith in Jesus Christ. So we have believed in Christ Jesus, that we might be accepted by God because of our faith in Christ—and not because we have obeyed the law. For no one will ever be saved by obeying the law.*

1 John 1:8-10 *If we say we have no sin, we are only fooling ourselves and refusing to accept the truth. But if we confess our sins to him, he is faithful and just to forgive us and to cleanse us from every wrong. If we claim we have not sinned, we are calling God a liar and showing that his word has no place in our hearts.* God's acceptance is not based on what we do, but on faith in Jesus Christ.

How can my faith help me accept circumstances I cannot change?

Romans 8:18, 23-25 *What we suffer now is nothing compared to the glory he will give us later. . . . Even we Christians, although we have the Holy Spirit within us as a foretaste of future glory, also groan to be released from pain and suffering. We, too, wait anxiously for that day when God will give us our full rights as his children, including the new bodies he has promised us. Now that we are saved, we eagerly look forward to this freedom. For if you already have something, you don't need to hope for it. But if we look forward to something we don't have yet, we must wait patiently and confidently.*

Job 2:10 *Job replied, ". . . Should we accept only good things from the hand of God and never anything bad?" So in all this, Job said nothing wrong.*

Ecclesiastes 5:19 *It is a good thing to receive wealth from God and the good health to enjoy it. To enjoy your work and accept your lot in life—that is indeed a gift from God.*

Luke 1:38 *Mary responded, "I am the Lord's servant, and I am willing to accept whatever he wants. May everything you have said come true."*

1 Corinthians 7:17 *You must accept whatever situation the Lord has put you in, and continue on as you were when God first called you. This is my rule for all the churches.*

Hebrews 10:34 *You suffered along with those who were thrown into jail. When all you owned was taken from you, you accepted it with joy. You knew you had better things waiting for you in eternity.* This is a fallen world, and Jesus' followers know better than to have unrealistic expectations. While we have hints of our future glory in Christ, we live amid the continuing trials of life. Accepting our circumstances doesn't mean we have to like them. By keeping eternity in mind we can grow from the difficulties we experience, knowing that difficult circumstances will end with this earthly life.

ADDICTION

see also Habit, Temptation

How can God break the power of addiction in my life?

Galatians 5:22-23 *When the Holy Spirit controls our lives, he will produce this kind of fruit in us: love, joy, peace, patience, kindness, goodness, faithfulness, gentleness, and self-control. Here there is no conflict with the law.*

Romans 8:5-9 *Those who are dominated by the sinful nature think about sinful things, but those who are controlled by the Holy Spirit think about things that please the Spirit. If your sinful nature controls your mind, there is death. But if the Holy Spirit controls your mind, there is life and peace. For the sinful nature is always hostile to God. It never did obey God's laws, and it never will. That's why those who are still under the control of their sinful nature can never please God. But you are not controlled by your sinful nature. You are controlled by the Spirit if you have the Spirit of God living in you. (And remember that those who do not have the Spirit of Christ living in them are not Christians at all.)*

God can break the power of addiction in your life when you give him control. He will come into your life and change your heart and your desires. Surrender to the Holy Spirit, and God will replace addictive drives with life-affirming desires.

Romans 12:2 *Don't copy the behavior and customs of this world, but let God transform you into a new person by changing the way you think. Then you will know what God wants you to do, and you will know how good and pleasing and perfect his will really is.*

1 John 4:4 *You belong to God, my dear children. You have already won your fight with these false prophets, because the Spirit who lives in you is greater than the spirit who lives in the world.*

1 John 5:4-5 *Every child of God defeats this evil world by trusting Christ to give the victory. And the ones who win this battle against the world are the ones who believe that Jesus is the Son of God.* Freedom comes as we change our focus and change our minds. We do this by trusting in Christ and experiencing the power he brings into our lives.

How do I ask God to help me be free of an addiction?

1 Peter 5:6-7 *Humble yourselves under the mighty power of God, and in his good time he will honor you. Give all your worries and cares to God, for he cares about what happens to you.* Admit your need to God in prayer, release all your anxieties to him, and rely fully on the promise of God's help.

ADULTERY

see Forgiveness, Temptation

ADVERSITY

see Challenges

AGE/AGING

Will God continue to be with me as I age?

Isaiah 46:4 *I will be your God throughout your lifetime—until your hair is white with age. I made you, and I will care for you. I will carry you along and save you.*
God's love lasts for all our days. This promise gives us a wonderful picture of God's care. He walks alongside us and carries us when we can no longer walk. In the end he will save us, bringing us through death to our final, glorious destination.

Will I still be useful in my old age?

Psalm 92:14 *Even in old age they will still produce fruit; they will remain vital and green.*
Regardless of our age, we can be productive and vital, telling others of God's goodness.

What can lead to a longer life?

Psalm 128:1, 6 *How happy are those who fear the LORD—all who follow his ways! . . . May you live to enjoy your grandchildren. And may Israel have quietness and peace.*

Proverbs 3:1-2 *My child, never forget the things I have taught you. Store my commands in your heart, for they will give you a long and satisfying life.*
Fear of the Lord, which involves knowing and obeying the Lord and his commands, leads to a satisfying life and often a long life as well. While there are times when a life is cut short by tragedy, the general rule is that knowing and obeying God lengthens life. Is it surprising that a close relationship with the author of life helps us enrich and lengthen our lives?

AGGRESSION

see Conflict

AIDS

see Suffering

ANGER

Is God angry with me?

Exodus 34:6-7 *He passed in front of Moses and said, "I am the LORD, I am the LORD, the merciful and gracious God. I am slow to anger and rich in unfailing love and faithfulness. I show this unfailing love to many thousands by forgiving every kind of sin and rebellion. Even so I do not leave sin unpunished, but I punish the children for the sins of their parents to the third and fourth generations."*

Psalm 7:10-11 *God is my shield, saving those whose hearts are true and right. God is a judge who is perfectly fair. He is angry with the wicked every day.*

Psalm 18:26-27 *To the pure you show yourself pure, but to the wicked you show yourself hostile. You rescue those who are humble, but you humiliate the proud.*

God cannot tolerate sin and rebellion against him. But he is ready to forgive, because he is kind and merciful. Those who humbly confess their sin and turn to him in faith receive God's abundant love and mercy instead of anger.

Psalm 30:5 *His anger lasts for a moment, but his favor lasts a lifetime! Weeping may go on all night, but joy comes with the morning.*

Psalm 145:8 *The LORD is kind and merciful, slow to get angry, full of unfailing love.*
The Bible promises that God is kind and merciful and always ready to welcome us into his love. The always-angry God is one of the worst caricatures ever attributed to God. God's anger toward his children is an expression of his love in action.

What can I do to reduce my angry responses?

1 Peter 2:21, 23 *Christ, who suffered for you, is your example. Follow in his steps. . . . He did not retaliate when he was insulted. When he suffered, he did not threaten to get even. He left his case in the hands of God, who always judges fairly.*
Jesus teaches that giving in to anger is giving up on God. Don't retaliate; trust God to handle the situation.

Proverbs 15:1 *A gentle answer turns away wrath, but harsh words stir up anger.*

Proverbs 29:8 *Mockers can get a whole town agitated, but those who are wise will calm anger.*
Giving in to anger gives even more power to the cause of our anger. Striking back invites the other person to strike back harder. Ask God to help you respond with gentleness and resist the urge to respond in anger.

Proverbs 19:11 *People with good sense restrain their anger; they earn esteem by overlooking wrongs.*

Psalm 4:4 *Don't sin by letting anger gain control over you. Think about it overnight and remain silent.* Anger is like mud: we can brush it off much better when it's dry. Don't react. Respond after you've had a chance to cool off and gain God's perspective.

ANXIETY

see Stress, Worry

ASSURANCE

How can I be assured of God's lasting care for me?

John 6:37 *However, those the Father has given me will come to me, and I will never reject them.*

John 10:28-30 *I give them eternal life, and they will never perish. No one will snatch them away from me, for my Father has given them to me, and he is more powerful than anyone else. So no one can take them from me. The Father and I are one.*

Lamentations 3:22-23 *The unfailing love of the LORD never ends! By his mercies we have been kept from complete destruction. Great is his faithfulness; his mercies begin afresh each day.*

Our confidence is rooted in God's hold on us, not our grip on God. His mercy and love are eternally new and never exhausted.

How can I be assured of God's love in difficult times?

Isaiah 43:1-2 *Now, O Israel, the LORD who created you says: "Do not be afraid, for I have ransomed you. I have called you by name; you are mine. When you go through deep waters and great trouble, I will be with you. When you go through rivers of difficulty, you will not drown! When you walk through the fire of oppression, you will not be burned up; the flames will not consume you."*

Romans 8:35, 38-39 *Can anything ever separate us from Christ's love? Does it mean he no longer loves us if we have trouble or calamity, or are persecuted, or are hungry or cold or in danger or threatened with death? . . . I am convinced that nothing can ever separate us from his love. Death can't, and life can't. The angels can't, and the demons can't. Our fears for today, our worries about tomorrow, and even the powers of hell can't keep God's love away. Whether we are high above the sky or in the deepest ocean, nothing in all creation will ever be able to separate us from the love of God that is revealed in Christ Jesus our Lord.*

Life's circumstances don't come between God and his people. They don't get in God's way. Hard times are often when God reveals his infinite love and care for us.

What does this assurance do for me when I confront everyday problems?

Hebrews 4:14-16 *We have a great High Priest who has gone to heaven, Jesus the Son of God. Let us cling to him and never stop trusting him. This High Priest of ours understands our weaknesses, for he faced all of the same temptations we do, yet he did not sin. So let us come boldly to the throne of our gracious God. There we will receive his mercy, and we will find grace to help us when we need it.*

Ephesians 3:12 *Because of Christ and our faith in him, we can now come fearlessly into God's presence, assured of his glad welcome.*
The assurance of God's love gives us courage to come to him with any problem, struggle, or concern. Our prayers are never interruptions to the Lord. When we knock, the door is always open to us.

ATTACKS

see Conflict

BACKSLIDING

see also Forgiveness, Guilt, Holy/Holiness

What do I do when I've fallen away from God?

Amos 5:4 *This is what the LORD says to the family of Israel: "Come back to me and live!"*

Romans 3:23-24 *All have sinned; all fall short of God's glorious standard. Yet now God in his gracious kindness declares us not guilty. He has done this through Christ Jesus, who has freed us by taking away our sins.*

Psalm 32:5 *Finally, I confessed all my sins to you and stopped trying to hide them. I said to myself, "I will confess my rebellion to the LORD." And you forgave me! All my guilt is gone.*

Because of our sinful nature, we might fall away from God. Yet once we've identified and confessed our sin, God is faithful to forgive us. There is no sin so great we cannot come back to God.

How can I avoid backsliding?

Ezekiel 37:23 *[Israel] will stop polluting themselves with their detestable idols and other sins, for I will save them from their sinful backsliding. I will cleanse them. Then they will truly be my people, and I will be their God.*

1 Peter 1:14 *Obey God because you are his children. Don't slip back into your old ways of doing evil; you didn't know any better then.*

Matthew 26:41 *Keep alert and pray. Otherwise temptation will overpower you. For though the spirit is willing enough, the body is weak!*

1 Corinthians 10:13 *Remember that the temptations that come into your life are no different from what others experience. And God is faithful. He will keep the temptation from becoming so strong that you can't stand up against it. When you are tempted, he will show you a way out so that you will not give in to it.*
Obedience to God's word, persistence in prayer, and resistance to temptation help us avoid backsliding.

BEGINNINGS

How do we get a new start?

2 Corinthians 5:17 *Those who become Christians become new persons. They are not the same anymore, for the old life is gone. A new life has begun!*
Those who believe in Jesus Christ are not simply turning over a new leaf; they are re-created as people! They have a new life.

How many opportunities does God give me to begin anew?

Lamentations 3:23 *Great is his faithfulness; his mercies begin afresh each day.*
We don't have to wait for New Year's resolutions to start over again. God renews his mercies to us every single day. We don't have to be burdened by yesterday's failures or regrets.

How can I know God is with me as I begin a new work?

Philippians 1:6 *I am sure that God, who began the good work within you, will continue his work until it is finally finished on that day when Christ Jesus comes back again.*
God has begun not only the work of salvation in us, but also the work of transforming every aspect of our lives. We invite him to work in our relationships, our work, our recreation, and every other part of our lives.

BELONGING

See also Relationships

What happens to those who belong to God?

Isaiah 26:19 *We have this assurance: Those who belong to God will live; their bodies will rise again! Those who sleep in the earth will rise up and sing for joy! For God's light of life will fall like dew on his people in the place of the dead!*

17

Belonging to God is an eternal relationship, not merely for this world, but for the world to come. The grave is not the last chapter, merely the transitional one.

John 15:9-17 *I have loved you even as the Father has loved me. Remain in my love. When you obey me, you remain in my love, just as I obey my Father and remain in his love. I have told you this so that you will be filled with my joy. Yes, your joy will overflow! I command you to love each other in the same way that I love you. And here is how to measure it—the greatest love is shown when people lay down their lives for their friends. You are my friends if you obey me. I no longer call you servants, because a master doesn't confide in his servants. Now you are my friends, since I have told you everything the Father told me. You didn't choose me. I chose you. I appointed you to go and produce fruit that will last, so that the Father will give you whatever you ask for, using my name. I command you to love each other.*

When we belong to God we belong to each other. Jesus' command to love is rooted in his promise of love for us. The fact that we belong to Jesus compels us to love one another. As friends of God we are responsible to all our fellow believers.

No one wants to be alone. How can I know I belong in fellowship with God's people?

Romans 12:4-5 *Just as our bodies have many parts and each part has a special function, so it is with Christ's body. We are all parts of his one body, and each of us has different work to do. And since we are all one body in Christ, we belong to each other, and each of us needs all the others.*

Belonging to God makes you part of Christ's body, the church. You belong in fellowship with God's people because you are in fellowship with God.

BETRAYAL

How do I handle betrayal—when someone hasn't been faithful to me?

Psalm 55:20-22 *As for this friend of mine, he betrayed me; he broke his promises. His words are as smooth as cream, but in his heart is war. His words are as soothing as lotion, but underneath are daggers! Give your burdens to the LORD, and he will take care of you. He will not permit the godly to slip and fall.*

Betrayal is like suddenly hitting a sheet of ice while driving. Our basis for trust is gone, and we go into a dangerous skid. But when we turn to the Lord, he throws sand on the road, restoring us to safety.

2 Timothy 2:13 *If we are unfaithful, he remains faithful, for he cannot deny himself.*

When others are unfaithful to us, we can take great comfort in God's unwavering faithfulness. We anchor our faith in the Lord, not in other frail human beings.

Where do we find the courage and strength to forgive our betrayer?

Romans 12:19-21 *Dear friends, never avenge yourselves. Leave that to God. For it is written, "I will take vengeance; I will repay those who deserve it," says the Lord. Instead, do what the Scriptures say: "If your enemies are hungry, feed them. If they are thirsty, give them something to drink, and they will be ashamed of what they have done to you." Don't let evil get the best of you, but conquer evil by doing good.*

The worst response to betrayal is to give in to vengeance. The wisest response to betrayal is to stop the cycle of retaliation and begin the strategy of blessing. Trust God to judge your cause.

Matthew 6:12-14 *Forgive us our sins, just as we have forgiven those who have sinned against us. And don't let us yield to temptation, but deliver us from the evil one. If you forgive those who sin against you, your heavenly Father will forgive you.*

Forgiveness is the only road to freedom. A forgiven person forgives. Nothing that anyone has done against us compares with what we have done against God. Refusing to forgive another means we don't realize just how much God has forgiven us.

BIBLE

What promises does the Bible contain and how can they affect us?

1 Peter 1:3-4 *All honor to the God and Father of our Lord Jesus Christ, for it is by his boundless mercy that God has given us the privilege of being born again. Now we live with a wonderful expectation because Jesus Christ rose again from the dead. For God has reserved a priceless inheritance for his children. It is kept in heaven for you, pure and undefiled, beyond the reach of change and decay.* The greatest promise in the Bible is God's forgiveness of our sins. We know this promise is true because Jesus rose from the dead. God promises his children that they will experience heaven forever.

What will happen when we implement the promises in God's word?

1 Peter 1:5-9 *God, in his mighty power, will protect you until you receive this salvation, because you are trusting him. It will be revealed on the last day for all to see. So be truly glad! There is wonderful joy ahead, even though it is necessary for you to endure many trials for a while. These trials are only to test your faith, to show that it is strong and pure. It is being tested as fire tests and purifies gold—and your faith is far more precious to God than mere gold. So if*

your faith remains strong after being tried by fiery trials, it will bring you much praise and glory and honor on the day when Jesus Christ is revealed to the whole world. You love him even though you have never seen him. Though you do not see him, you trust him; and even now you are happy with a glorious, inexpressible joy. Your reward for trusting him will be the salvation of your souls.

When we take God at his word, we enter into the fullness of life in Christ. We trust his ways and obey them. We trust his provision and are content and patient. We rely on the promise of his love and are able to love others as we have been loved. God's promises pave the pathway of discipleship.

What is promised to us when we study the Bible?

Jeremiah 15:16 *Your words are what sustain me. They bring me great joy and are my heart's delight, for I bear your name, O LORD God Almighty.*
The Bible sustains and directs us physically, mentally, emotionally, and spiritually, bringing lasting joy and deep satisfaction in life.

John 8:32 *You will know the truth, and the truth will set you free.*
Reading the Bible tells us how to be set free from sin.

22

Deuteronomy 17:19-20 *[The king] must always keep this copy of the law with him and read it daily as long as he lives. That way he will learn to fear the LORD his God by obeying all the terms of this law. This regular reading will prevent him from becoming proud and acting as if he is above his fellow citizens. It will also prevent him from turning away from these commands in the smallest way. This will ensure that he and his descendants will reign for many generations in Israel.*
Reading the Bible helps us keep a right attitude toward God and others.

Psalm 119:9 *How can a young person stay pure? By obeying your word and following its rules.*
Reading the Bible can help us know how to keep pure.

Psalm 119:24 *Your decrees please me; they give me wise advice.*

Proverbs 6:22 *Wherever you walk, their counsel can lead you. When you sleep, they will protect you. When you wake up in the morning, they will advise you.*

Psalm 119:19 *I am but a foreigner here on earth; I need the guidance of your commands. Don't hide them from me!*

Psalm 119:105 *Your word is a lamp for my feet and a light for my path.*

Reading the Bible guides us in daily living, giving us the best counsel for our problems.

P s a l m   1 1 9 : 5 0 *Your promise revives me; it comforts me in all my troubles.*
Reading the Bible gives us hope for the future.

P s a l m   1 1 9 : 5 2 *I meditate on your age-old laws; O LORD, they comfort me.*
Reading the Bible gives us comfort.

BLESSINGS

How has God promised to bless his people?

N u m b e r s   6 : 2 4 - 2 6 *May the LORD bless you and protect you. May the LORD smile on you and be gracious to you. May the LORD show you his favor and give you his peace.*
God's blessing encompasses all of life. We live in his protection, his presence, and his peace. Nothing this world offers can compare in scope or duration with the blessing of God.

J e r e m i a h   1 7 : 7 *Blessed are those who trust in the LORD and have made the LORD their hope and confidence.*
We are tempted to base our hope and confidence on worldly circumstances such as a good job or financial security. But these cannot compare to the promises that we have in God, the creator of heaven and earth. Put your hope where it cannot and will not be shaken.

24

2 Corinthians 12:13 *The only thing I didn't do, which I do in the other churches, was to become a burden to you. Please forgive me for this wrong!*
Jesus Christ blesses us with forgiveness and redemption. God the Father blesses us with the assurance that we are loved and of infinite worth. The Holy Spirit blesses us with fellowship and the continual presence of God.

Can we do things that affect how much God blesses us?

Psalm 84:11 *The LORD God is our light and protector. He gives us grace and glory. No good thing will the LORD withhold from those who do what is right.*
God promises to bless those who do what is right; he doesn't extend the same promise to those who don't do what is right.

Proverbs 19:17 *If you help the poor, you are lending to the LORD—and he will repay you!*
God promises to bless those who help the poor.

How does the promise of blessing affect us when we are weary or discouraged?

1 Corinthians 15:57-58 *How we thank God, who gives us victory over sin and death through Jesus Christ our Lord! So, my dear brothers and sisters, be strong and steady, always enthusiastic about the Lord's work, for you know that nothing you do for the Lord is ever useless.*

Galatians 6:9 *Don't get tired of doing what is good. Don't get discouraged and give up, for we will reap a harvest of blessing at the appropriate time.* When we are tempted to give up, new resolve comes from remembering that God promises to bring a harvest in his perfect time.

BOLDNESS

see Courage

BROKENHEARTED

see Encouragement, Comfort

BURNOUT

see also Busyness, Stress, Time

Is something wrong with me if I am burning out?

Isaiah 40:29-31 *He gives power to those who are tired and worn out; he offers strength to the weak. Even youths will become exhausted, and young men will give up. But those who wait on the LORD will find new strength. They will fly high on wings like eagles. They will run and not grow weary. They will walk and not faint.* Spiritual, mental, physical, and emotional exhaustion are natural consequences of being human, especially for those who give themselves wholeheartedly to God's service. But they are not permanent conditions. To wait on the Lord means to stop trying to force things to happen and start trusting his timing.

How can I find new joy and energy?

Isaiah 30:15 *The Sovereign LORD, the Holy One of Israel, says, "Only in returning to me and waiting for me will you be saved. In quietness and confidence is your strength."*
Burnout comes when we lose our connection to the Lord. When we live out of our love for him, we experience his strength working through us.

Matthew 11:28-29 *Jesus said, "Come to me, all of you who are weary and carry heavy burdens, and I will give you rest. Take my yoke upon you. Let me teach you, because I am humble and gentle, and you will find rest for your souls."*
Burnout often comes when we take too much responsibility on ourselves. When we put our confidence in the Lord, the burden lightens.

BUSYNESS

see also Burnout, Stress, Time

Does God expect me to be busy all the time?

Psalm 23:2 *He lets me rest in green meadows; he leads me beside peaceful streams.*

Matthew 11:28-29 *Jesus said, "Come to me, all*

of you who are weary and carry heavy burdens, and I will give you rest. Take my yoke upon you. Let me teach you, because I am humble and gentle, and you will find rest for your souls."

Activity itself is not a virtue; it can actually be a detriment to our spiritual lives. The Lord invites us to rest and be refreshed in his care.

What is the antidote to empty busyness?

Psalm 90:12 *Teach us to make the most of our time, so that we may grow in wisdom.*

Ephesians 5:15-20 *Be careful how you live, not as fools but as those who are wise. Make the most of every opportunity for doing good in these evil days. Don't act thoughtlessly, but try to understand what the Lord wants you to do. Don't be drunk with wine, because that will ruin your life. Instead, let the Holy Spirit fill and control you. Then you will sing psalms and hymns and spiritual songs among yourselves, making music to the Lord in your hearts. And you will always give thanks for everything to God the Father in the name of our Lord Jesus Christ.*

The key to overcoming empty busyness is to live wisely for God. God empowers us to make the most of the time he's given us.

CALL OF GOD

see also Will of God

Is God calling me to serve him?

1 Corinthians 12:4-7 *There are different kinds of spiritual gifts, but it is the same Holy Spirit who is the source of them all. There are different kinds of service in the church, but it is the same Lord we are serving. There are different ways God works in our lives, but it is the same God who does the work through all of us. A spiritual gift is given to each of us as a means of helping the entire church.*

God's call is based on his promise of the Holy Spirit at work in our lives. Each of us is called to serve the Lord with the gifts we've been given.

Can I lose God's call?

Romans 11:29 *God's gifts and his call can never be withdrawn.*

God's call is like our family name. Even when we feel like we've dishonored our family, we do not lose our name. Likewise, God promises to use us as we persevere in our faith.

What does God provide so I can fulfill his call?

Hebrews 13:20-21 *Now, may the God of peace, who brought again from the dead our Lord Jesus, equip you with all you need for doing his will. May he* produce in you, through the power of Jesus Christ, all that is pleasing to him. Jesus is the great Shepherd of the sheep by an everlasting covenant, signed with his blood. To him be glory forever and ever. Amen.

Where God calls, he equips. The power of the resurrected Lord ensures that we fulfill God's call in our lives.

CHALLENGES

Why does God allow challenges in our lives?

James 1:2-4 *Dear brothers and sisters, whenever trouble comes your way, let it be an opportunity for joy. For when your faith is tested, your endurance has a chance to grow. So let it grow, for when your endurance is fully developed, you will be strong in character and ready for anything.*

Challenges that threaten and try us are the very tools that God uses to strengthen and mature us. As we endure, we gain greater wisdom, integrity, and courage to face whatever comes our way.

Are some challenges too small to bother God?

Psalm 37:5 *Commit everything you do to the LORD. Trust him, and he will help you.*

Nothing is too small for God. When we commit our plans to the Lord, he commits himself and his infinite resources to us.

What has God given me to help me face my challenges?

Joshua 1:7 *Be strong and very courageous. Obey all the laws Moses gave you. Do not turn away from them, and you will be successful in everything you do.* God has given us his word to direct us. The promise of success is embedded in our commitment to obedience.

1 Chronicles 28:20 *David continued, "Be strong and courageous, and do the work. Don't be afraid or discouraged by the size of the task, for the LORD God, my God, is with you. He will not fail you or forsake you. He will see to it that all the work related to the Temple of the LORD is finished correctly."* Instead of being discouraged by the size of the task, we should be encouraged by the limitless power of God.

CHANGE

Where can I find security and hope in the midst of tumult and change?

Lamentations 5:19 *LORD, you remain the same forever! Your throne continues from generation to generation.*

Malachi 3:6 *I am the LORD, and I do not change. That is why you descendants of Jacob are not already completely destroyed.*

James 1:17 *Whatever is good and perfect comes to us from God above, who created all heaven's lights. Unlike them, he never changes or casts shifting shadows.*

Hebrews 13:8 *Jesus Christ is the same yesterday, today, and forever.*
Both our security and our hope are rooted in God's unchanging character. People will make promises one day but disappoint us the next. Sin or circumstances beyond their control prevent them from keeping their promises. God's faithfulness and love, however, are not subject to the fluctuations of time, space, or human mortality. We will never suffer because of God's fickle whims, irrational mood swings, or inability to handle the circumstances.

Are there any unchanging principles that can help me stay anchored?

Isaiah 40:8 *The grass withers, and the flowers fade, but the word of our God stands forever.*

Mark 13:31 *Heaven and earth will disappear, but my words will remain forever.*
God's word gives us the truth that never changes. We find strength and courage when we listen— not to the voices of public opinion—but to God.

Are there some changes that are too overwhelming for our faith?

Psalm 46:1-2 *God is our refuge and strength,
always ready to help in times of trouble. So we will
not fear, even if earthquakes come and the mountains
crumble into the sea.*
Faith is the answer to fear. No amount of change
in our life will affect God's care for us.

How can I hope that I can change for the better?

2 Corinthians 5:17 *Those who become
Christians become new persons. They are not the same
anymore, for the old life is gone. A new life has
begun!*

Philippians 1:6 *I am sure that God, who began
the good work within you, will continue his work until
it is finally finished on that day when Christ Jesus
comes back again.*
A great work takes a long time to complete.
Though we are converted in a moment of faith,
the process of transformation into Christ-likeness
takes a lifetime. While it may appear slow to us, it
is relentless and certain.

CHARACTER

see also Holy/Holiness

Will God do anything to change my character, or is it all up to me?

Galatians 5:22-23 *When the Holy Spirit controls our lives, he will produce this kind of fruit in us: love, joy, peace, patience, kindness, goodness, faithfulness, gentleness, and self-control. Here there is no conflict with the law.*

Philippians 2:5, 12-13 *Your attitude should be the same that Christ Jesus had. . . . Dearest friends, you were always so careful to follow my instructions when I was with you. And now that I am away you must be even more careful to put into action God's saving work in your lives, obeying God with deep reverence and fear. For God is working in you, giving you the desire to obey him and the power to do what pleases him.*

A transformed character reflects God's work within us and our own choices. The Holy Spirit awakens our desire for love, integrity, and responsibility, but we must choose these in every situation.

What does God promise as we mature in godly character?

Matthew 5:8 *God blesses those whose hearts are pure, for they will see God.*

We will experience an increasing sense of God's presence and his blessing.

James 1:4 *When your endurance is fully developed, you will be strong in character and ready for anything.*

Romans 5:3-5 *We can rejoice, too, when we run into problems and trials, for we know that they are good for us—they help us learn to endure. And endurance develops strength of character in us, and character strengthens our confident expectation of salvation. And this expectation will not disappoint us. For we know how dearly God loves us, because he has given us the Holy Spirit to fill our hearts with his love.*

As we mature in our faith, we will become stronger and stronger people. Character is like a muscle—it gets stronger with exercise. As our character develops, our confidence in our salvation increases, and the assurance of God's love fills our hearts.

CHILDREN

see Family

CHRISTLIKENESS

How can I ever expect to be like Jesus?

2 Corinthians 3:18 *All of us have had that veil removed so that we can be mirrors that brightly reflect the glory of the Lord. And as the Spirit of the Lord works within us, we become more and more like him and reflect his glory even more.*

When we trust in Christ for salvation, he begins to work in our hearts. As the Spirit works within us, he changes us to be more and more like Jesus.

Galatians 2:20 *I myself no longer live, but Christ lives in me. So I live my life in this earthly body by trusting in the Son of God, who loved me and gave himself for me.*

John 14:12-14 *The truth is, anyone who believes in me will do the same works I have done, and even greater works, because I am going to be with the Father. You can ask for anything in my name, and I will do it, because the work of the Son brings glory to the Father. Yes, ask anything in my name, and I will do it!*

We should not simply ask for things from the Lord; we should ask to be like the Lord. We have the amazing promise that we can become like him and do what he has done!

What does the future hold for those who trust in Jesus Christ?

1 John 3:2-3 *Yes, dear friends, we are already God's children, and we can't even imagine what we will be like when Christ returns. But we do know that when he comes we will be like him, for we will see him as he really is. And all who believe this will keep themselves pure, just as Christ is pure.*

We are like Christ in that we are children of God, but we will not be completely like him until we leave this temporal world. The promise of becoming like Jesus motivates us to live a pure life in body and mind.

CHURCH

Do we really need the church?

Ephesians 1:19-23 *I pray that you will begin to understand the incredible greatness of his power for us who believe him. This is the same mighty power that raised Christ from the dead and seated him in the place of honor at God's right hand in the heavenly realms. Now he is far above any ruler or authority or power or leader or anything else in this world or in the world to come. And God has put all things under the authority of Christ, and he gave him this authority for the benefit of the church. And the church is his body; it is filled by Christ, who fills everything everywhere with his presence.* God wants to do great things in the church. The people of God are equipped with the resurrection power of Jesus Christ and are the emissaries of the Lord who rules over all! When we come together with this vision, we have confidence that God will do more than we could have ever imagined.

But sometimes the church seems so weak. How can we have hope for the church?

Matthew 16:18 *Upon this rock I will build my church, and all the powers of hell will not conquer it.* The church will not be overcome; Jesus promises that he will build his church. The Lord is using the church as his divine instrument to overcome evil with good.

Can God work through the church to help me?

James 5:14-15 *Are any among you sick? They should call for the elders of the church and have them pray over them, anointing them with oil in the name of the Lord. And their prayer offered in faith will heal the sick, and the Lord will make them well. And anyone who has committed sins will be forgiven.*
God's promises draw us into fellowship with God's people. He works through the church in order to deepen our love and support for one another.

COMFORT

How does God comfort us?

Psalm 23:4 *Even when I walk through the dark valley of death, I will not be afraid, for you are close beside me. Your rod and your staff protect and comfort me.*

Psalm 30:5 *His anger lasts for a moment, but his favor lasts a lifetime! Weeping may go on all night, but joy comes with the morning.*

Matthew 5:4 *God blesses those who mourn, for they will be comforted.*
God comforts us by staying close beside us in difficulty, by blessing us even when we are in mourning, and by promising us joy to come.

Psalm 34:18 *The LORD is close to the brokenhearted; he rescues those who are crushed in spirit.*

Psalm 147:3 *He heals the brokenhearted, binding up their wounds.*
God comforts us by healing our hearts, even when they are broken.

Exodus 14:13 *Moses told the people, "Don't be afraid. Just stand where you are and watch the LORD rescue you. The Egyptians that you see today will never be seen again."*

Psalm 145:14 *The LORD helps the fallen and lifts up those bent beneath their loads.*

John 16:33 *I have told you all this so that you may have peace in me. Here on earth you will have many trials and sorrows. But take heart, because I have overcome the world.*

Isaiah 41:10 *Don't be afraid, for I am with you. Do not be dismayed, for I am your God. I will strengthen you. I will help you. I will uphold you with my victorious right hand.*
When we are overwhelmed, God comforts us with his presence. He calms our hearts, renews our confidence, and awakens our hope.

Will God really take time to involve himself in my little problems?

Isaiah 40:11 *He will feed his flock like a shepherd. He will carry the lambs in his arms, holding them close to his heart. He will gently lead the mother sheep with their young.*

Luke 12:6-7 *What is the price of five sparrows? A couple of pennies? Yet God does not forget a single one of them. And the very hairs on your head are all numbered. So don't be afraid; you are more valuable to him than a whole flock of sparrows.*

1 Peter 5:7 *Give all your worries and cares to God, for he cares about what happens to you.*
God measures problems by love, not by size. Even small things can be avenues for God's great care. Don't look at the size of your problem but look at the greatness of God's love and concern.

How can the Bible give me comfort?

Psalm 119:49-50, 52, 54 *Remember your promise to me, for it is my only hope. Your promise revives me; it comforts me in all my troubles. . . . I meditate on your age-old laws; O LORD, they comfort me. . . . Your principles have been the music of my life throughout the years of my pilgrimage.*

Proverbs 30:5 *Every word of God proves true. He defends all who come to him for protection.*

Romans 15:4 *Such things were written in the Scriptures long ago to teach us. They give us hope and encouragement as we wait patiently for God's promises.*

God's promises in the Bible comfort and encourage us in this life and give us the confident assurance that we will one day live forever in peace and security with him.

How can we comfort others?

2 Corinthians 1:3-4 *All praise to the God and Father of our Lord Jesus Christ. He is the source of every mercy and the God who comforts us. He comforts us in all our troubles so that we can comfort others. When others are troubled, we will be able to give them the same comfort God has given us.*
God helps us comfort others in the ways that he comforts us. When we have experienced God's assuring love, his guiding wisdom, and his sustaining power, we are able to approach others with similar empathy and conviction.

What is my greatest comfort?

John 3:16 *God so loved the world that he gave his only Son, so that everyone who believes in him will not perish but have eternal life.*

John 6:37 *Those the Father has given me will come to me, and I will never reject them.*

2 Thessalonians 2:16-17 *May our Lord Jesus Christ and God our Father, who loved us and in his special favor gave us everlasting comfort and good hope, comfort your hearts and give you strength in every good thing you do and say.*

Our greatest comfort is knowing that we are saved from sin and will live eternally with God. In heaven, all sin and fear and trouble will have disappeared.

CONFESSION

see Forgiveness

CONFIDENCE

see also Hope

Where do we find confidence for every day?

Psalm 27:1 *The LORD is my light and my salvation—so why should I be afraid? The LORD protects me from danger—so why should I tremble?*

Psalm 121:8 *The LORD keeps watch over you as you come and go, both now and forever.*

John 16:33 *I have told you all this so that you may have peace in me. Here on earth you will have many trials and sorrows. But take heart, because I have overcome the world.*

Many of the greatest athletes say that their real contest is a mental, not a physical one. It's the same way in our spiritual life. Our confidence comes not from looking around at our physical circumstances, but from looking to God.

How can we have confidence in the face of life's greatest hardships?

Proverbs 3:5-6 *Trust in the LORD with all your heart; do not depend on your own understanding. Seek his will in all you do, and he will direct your paths.* When we rely on God, he will not let us down. Our limited understanding is no match for his limitless love and grace.

Romans 8:38-39 *I am convinced that nothing can ever separate us from his love. Death can't, and life can't. The angels can't, and the demons can't. Our fears for today, our worries about tomorrow, and even the powers of hell can't keep God's love away. Whether we are high above the sky or in the deepest ocean, nothing in all creation will ever be able to separate us from the love of God that is revealed in Christ Jesus our Lord.*

Philippians 4:11-13 *Not that I was ever in need, for I have learned how to get along happily whether I have much or little. I know how to live on almost nothing or with everything. I have learned the secret of living in every situation, whether it is with a full stomach or empty, with plenty or little. For I can do everything with the help of Christ who gives me the strength I need.*
Our happiness rises and falls, but our steady confidence comes from the consistency of Christ. We depend on Christ—not on circumstances.

Is there anything I can do to cultivate greater confidence?

Psalm 112:5-8 *All goes well for those who are generous, who lend freely and conduct their business fairly. Such people will not be overcome by evil circumstances. Those who are righteous will be long remembered. They do not fear bad news; they confidently trust the LORD to care for them. They are confident and fearless and can face their foes triumphantly.* Following God's principles gives us the confidence of a clear conscience.

CONFLICT

see also Anger

Shouldn't those who believe in Jesus Christ be free from conflict?

Psalm 27:1-3 *The LORD is my light and my salvation—so why should I be afraid? The LORD protects me from danger—so why should I tremble? When evil people come to destroy me, when my enemies and foes attack me, they will stumble and fall. Though a mighty army surrounds me, my heart will know no fear. Even if they attack me, I remain confident.* Evil is inevitable. Because we live in a fallen world filled with broken people, we will find ourselves in many types of conflict. Our focus should not be on the dark forces that attack us but on the Lord who defends us.

Psalm 55:18 *He rescues me and keeps me safe from the battle waged against me, even though many still oppose me.*
While God doesn't keep us out of all conflict, he is present with us in it.

How can I find strength to respond to conflict in God's way?

Matthew 5:9 *God blesses those who work for peace, for they will be called the children of God.*

Romans 12:19-21 *Dear friends, never avenge yourselves. Leave that to God. For it is written, "I will take vengeance; I will repay those who deserve it," says the Lord. Instead, do what the Scriptures say: "If your enemies are hungry, feed them. If they are thirsty, give them something to drink, and they will be ashamed of what they have done to you." Don't let evil get the best of you, but conquer evil by doing good.*

1 Peter 3:9-12 *Don't repay evil for evil. Don't retaliate when people say unkind things about you. Instead, pay them back with a blessing. That is what God wants you to do, and he will bless you for it. For the Scriptures say, "If you want a happy life and good days, keep your tongue from speaking evil, and keep your lips from telling lies. Turn away from evil and do good. Work hard at living in peace with others. The eyes of the Lord watch over those who do right, and his ears are open to their prayers. But the Lord turns his face against those who do evil."*

Peace lies in the power of love, not the love of power. If we trust in God, he promises to protect and vindicate us. Followers of Christ know better than to take revenge into their own hands. They know that fighting according to the world's ways brings even greater problems. We are to practice "the principle of paradox": bless when cursed, give when threatened, and feed those who would take our food. This principle unleashes God's power into the situation.

CONTENTMENT

How can I experience contentment?

1 Timothy 6:6-7 *True religion with contentment is great wealth. After all, we didn't bring anything with us when we came into the world, and we certainly cannot carry anything with us when we die.*

Isaiah 26:3 *You will keep in perfect peace all who trust in you, whose thoughts are fixed on you!* Contentment begins with realizing our eternal destiny. It isn't how much we own, but where we are headed. When we realize that there is more to life than our time on earth, everything takes on a new value.

Hebrews 13:5 *Stay away from the love of money; be satisfied with what you have. For God has said, "I will never fail you. I will never forsake you."*

Contentment settles in our hearts when we meditate on God's presence and his priorities for our lives. Money and material goods cannot offer the peace and satisfaction that God offers. The richest people on earth, in material terms, are impoverished if they have no treasures in heaven. Those who have an inheritance in heaven are truly rich.

Philippians 4:11-13 *I have learned how to get along happily whether I have much or little. I know how to live on almost nothing or with everything. I have learned the secret of living in every situation, whether it is with a full stomach or empty, with plenty or little. For I can do everything with the help of Christ who gives me the strength I need.*

2 Peter 1:3 *As we know Jesus better, his divine power gives us everything we need for living a godly life. He has called us to receive his own glory and goodness!*
When we have Jesus Christ, we have all we need. He teaches us to discern the valuable things in life from the distractions. Contentment comes from being in Christ's presence, not from accumulating worldly possessions.

How can we find freedom from the sins of comparison, competition, and jealousy that disturb our contentment?

Psalm 23:1-3 *The LORD is my shepherd; I have everything I need. He lets me rest in green meadows; he leads me beside peaceful streams. He renews my strength. He guides me along right paths, bringing honor to his name.*

Contentment is found in God's continual care for us. The opening verses of this beloved psalm remind us that God guards us with his love, rest, protection, provision, and direction. Nothing else in this world can satisfy us as deeply and completely.

John 21:20-22 *Peter turned around and saw the disciple Jesus loved following them—the one who had leaned over to Jesus during supper and asked, "Lord, who among us will betray you?" Peter asked Jesus, "What about him, Lord?" Jesus replied, "If I want him to remain alive until I return, what is that to you? You follow me."*

Comparison robs us of peace and contentment. Jesus calls us to travel our own unique road with him. We will find joy and satisfaction when we resist comparing ourselves to others and focus on following him.

COURAGE

see also Fear

Where do I turn when I'm afraid?

Joshua 1:9 *I command you—be strong and courageous! Do not be afraid or discouraged. For the* LORD *your God is with you wherever you go.*

Psalm 27:1 *The* LORD *is my light and my salvation—so why should I be afraid? The* LORD *protects me from danger—so why should I tremble?*

Isaiah 41:10 *Don't be afraid, for I am with you. Do not be dismayed, for I am your God. I will strengthen you. I will help you. I will uphold you with my victorious right hand.*

Courage comes from trusting the presence of God. Fear comes from feeling alone against a great threat. The Lord promises that we are never alone. Meditate on his presence not on the problem.

Are there models of courage that can inspire me?

Hebrews 12:1-3 *Since we are surrounded by such a huge crowd of witnesses to the life of faith, let us strip off every weight that slows us down, especially the sin that so easily hinders our progress. And let us run with endurance the race that God has set before us. We do this by keeping our eyes on Jesus, on whom our faith depends from start to finish. He was willing to die a shameful death on the cross because of the joy he knew would be his afterward. Now he is seated in the place of highest honor beside God's throne in heaven. Think about all he endured when sinful people did such terrible things to him, so that you don't become weary and give up.*

Courage comes from following Christ. While God's presence is our greatest encouragement, we also have the courageous examples of those who have gone before us (see Hebrews 11). Above all, we gain great strength when we meditate on Jesus' courage. He showed that looking to our eternal reward gets us through the worst temporal trials.

Will God take away the things that frighten me?

Acts 4:24, 29-31 *All the believers were united as they lifted their voices in prayer: . . . "O Lord, hear their threats, and give your servants great boldness in their preaching. Send your healing power; may miraculous signs and wonders be done through the name of your holy servant Jesus." After this prayer, the building where they were meeting shook, and they were all filled with the Holy Spirit. And they preached God's message with boldness.*

Courage comes from the Holy Spirit. The early church was constantly threatened by the religious leaders in Jerusalem. They did not pray for the threats to end but for the courage to face those threats. The Holy Spirit gives us the boldness to turn threats into opportunities for testifying to our faith.

Job 11:18 *You will have courage because you will have hope. You will be protected and will rest in safety.*
Hope helps us see beyond the immediate crisis. Our hope is fixed on God's enduring promises, not temporary problems.

CRISIS

Shouldn't those who believe in God be free from crisis?

John 16:33 *I have told you all this so that you may have peace in me. Here on earth you will have many trials and sorrows. But take heart, because I have overcome the world.*
Crisis should not surprise us. We expect crisis and difficulty because we live in a fallen world. Jesus' warning keeps us from panic, and his promise of victory keeps us from discouragement.

Psalm 46:1-3 *God is our refuge and strength, always ready to help in times of trouble. So we will not fear, even if earthquakes come and the mountains crumble into the sea. Let the oceans roar and foam. Let the mountains tremble as the waters surge!*
Nothing in this world is stable or safe. We can find no lasting shelter apart from the Lord. When we rely on him, though everything else is shaken, our faith never will never be.

Psalm 50:15 *Trust me in your times of trouble, and I will rescue you, and you will give me glory.*
God promises to rescue us for our own welfare and for his glory.

What happens to us through times of crisis?

Romans 5:3-4 *We can rejoice, too, when we run into problems and trials, for we know that they are good for us—they help us learn to endure. And endurance develops strength of character in us, and character strengthens our confident expectation of salvation.*
God's transforming power often touches us most deeply in times of crisis. Times of crisis can strengthen our character.

2 Corinthians 12:10 *Since I know it is all for Christ's good, I am quite content with my weaknesses and with insults, hardships, persecutions, and calamities. For when I am weak, then I am strong.*
Spiritual strength can grow from physical weakness. Being physically weak teaches us that we cannot rely on our own strength to see us through—we need God's strength.

1 Peter 1:6-7 *Be truly glad! There is wonderful joy ahead, even though it is necessary for you to endure many trials for a while. These trials are only to test your faith, to show that it is strong and pure. It is*

being tested as fire tests and purifies gold—and your faith is far more precious to God than mere gold. So if your faith remains strong after being tried by fiery trials, it will bring you much praise and glory and honor on the day when Jesus Christ is revealed to the whole world.

Times of crisis are like a fire that refines, like a knife that prunes, like a wind that sifts the wheat from the chaff. Ask God for the strength to hold on and for the strength to let go of ungodly things. Look to the joy that awaits on the other side of the trial.

DANGER

see Crisis, Rescue

DEATH/DYING

Is death the end of all hope?

John 14:2 *There are many rooms in my Father's home, and I am going to prepare a place for you. If this were not so, I would tell you plainly.*

When we travel, it's comforting to know there's a place to stay at the end of the day. This same comfort is ours as we think of the end of this life. Though death is a great unknown, Jesus Christ has gone before us. He has prepared a glorious place for us to stay.

John 11:25 *Jesus told her, "I am the resurrection and the life. Those who believe in me, even though they die like everyone else, will live again."*

Romans 8:10-11 *Since Christ lives within you, even though your body will die because of sin, your spirit is alive because you have been made right with God. The Spirit of God, who raised Jesus from the dead, lives in you. And just as he raised Christ from the dead, he will give life to your mortal body by this same Spirit living within you.*

Physical death is not the end, it is but a stage in life. Physical death is the door to eternal life for those who believe in Jesus Christ. Those who believe are promised a glorious future—the resurrection of the body and everlasting life.

What is the hope for those who trust Jesus Christ as Savior?

Romans 6:23 *The wages of sin is death, but the free gift of God is eternal life through Christ Jesus our Lord.* Death is the consequence of sin, but Christ died in our place so he might give us eternal life. That gift is ours through faith.

Romans 10:9-10 *If you confess with your mouth that Jesus is Lord and believe in your heart that God raised him from the dead, you will be saved. For it is by believing in your heart that you are made right with God, and it is by confessing with your mouth that you are saved.*

Believing that Jesus Christ is the resurrected son of God who died in our place saves us from eternal death. This is our comfort and hope.

Romans 8:10 *Since Christ lives within you, even though your body will die because of sin, your spirit is alive because you have been made right with God.* We have hope because Jesus Christ defeated death!

What will happen to us when we die?

2 Corinthians 5:1-10 *We know that when this earthly tent we live in is taken down—when we die and leave these bodies—we will have a home in heaven, an eternal body made for us by God himself and not by human hands. We grow weary in our present bodies, and we long for the day when we will put on our heavenly bodies like new clothing. For we will not be spirits without bodies, but we will put on new heavenly bodies. Our dying bodies make us groan and sigh, but it's not that we want to die and have no bodies at all. We want to slip into our new bodies so that these dying bodies will be swallowed up by everlasting life. God himself has prepared us for this, and as a guarantee he has given us his Holy Spirit. So we are always confident, even though we know that as long as we live in these bodies we are not at home with the Lord. That is why we live by believing and not by seeing. Yes, we are fully confident, and we would rather be away from these bodies, for then we*

will be at home with the Lord. So our aim is to please him always, whether we are here in this body or away from this body. For we must all stand before Christ to be judged. We will each receive whatever we deserve for the good or evil we have done in our bodies.

Isaiah 25:7-8 *In that day he will remove the cloud of gloom, the shadow of death that hangs over the earth. He will swallow up death forever! The Sovereign LORD will wipe away all tears. He will remove forever all insults and mockery against his land and people. The LORD has spoken!*

1 Corinthians 15:53-57 *Our perishable earthly bodies must be transformed into heavenly bodies that will never die. When this happens—when our perishable earthly bodies have been transformed into heavenly bodies that will never die—then at last the Scriptures will come true: "Death is swallowed up in victory. O death, where is your victory? O death, where is your sting?" For sin is the sting that results in death, and the law gives sin its power. How we thank God, who gives us victory over sin and death through Jesus Christ our Lord!*

What an adventure awaits those who trust in Jesus Christ! Our bodies will be totally transformed into bodies that will never again be subjected to sin, pain, and the limitations of this world.

DECISIONS

see also Guidance, Will of God

What do we do when we don't know what to do?

2 Chronicles 20:12 *O our God, won't you stop them? We are powerless against this mighty army that is about to attack us. We do not know what to do, but we are looking to you for help.*
We don't have to know what to do, but we do need to know where to look. As the saying goes, it isn't so much what we know, but *who* we know!

Proverbs 3:5-7 *Trust in the LORD with all your heart; do not depend on your own understanding. Seek his will in all you do, and he will direct your paths. Don't be impressed with your own wisdom. Instead, fear the LORD and turn your back on evil.*
Trust the Lord to direct your steps, even when the way is confusing. God will guide you.

What kind of help does God give us?

2 Chronicles 16:9 *The eyes of the LORD search the whole earth in order to strengthen those whose hearts are fully committed to him.*
God wants to help us make the right decisions. He is looking for us to depend fully on him. Our openness is God's opportunity.

James 1:5-8 *If you need wisdom—if you want to know what God wants you to do—ask him, and he will gladly tell you. He will not resent your asking. But when you ask him, be sure that you really expect him to answer, for a doubtful mind is as unsettled as a wave of the sea that is driven and tossed by the wind. People like that should not expect to receive anything from the Lord. They can't make up their minds. They waver back and forth in everything they do.*

Some people fear that they are bothering God with their problems. Nothing could be further from the truth. God is looking for ways to help us because he loves us. Our commitment to him releases his resources for us.

Romans 8:26-27 *The Holy Spirit helps us in our distress. For we don't even know what we should pray for, nor how we should pray. But the Holy Spirit prays for us with groanings that cannot be expressed in words. And the Father who knows all hearts knows what the Spirit is saying, for the Spirit pleads for us believers in harmony with God's own will.*

When we are overwhelmed, confused, or uncertain, we should not hesitate to pray. In fact, these are the best times to pray because the Holy Spirit can then help us the most. We describe our situation and trust God to prescribe the solution.

DEPRESSION

What can I do when I'm depressed?

Psalm 42:5-6 *Why am I discouraged? Why so sad? I will put my hope in God! I will praise him again—my Savior and my God! Now I am deeply discouraged, but I will remember your kindness—from Mount Hermon, the source of the Jordan, from the land of Mount Mizar.*

Depression is a time for soul-searching, for asking basic questions. We are often discouraged because we concentrate on our circumstances instead of on the Lord who will always care for us. The psalmist's questions awakened him to the reality that God alone is our source of comfort and hope. When we are depressed, we need to remind ourselves that God has been faithful in the past and will be faithful in the present.

Habakkuk 3:17-19 *Even though the fig trees have no blossoms, and there are no grapes on the vine; even though the olive crop fails, and the fields lie empty and barren; even though the flocks die in the fields, and the cattle barns are empty, yet I will rejoice in the LORD! I will be joyful in the God of my salvation. The Sovereign LORD is my strength! He will make me as surefooted as a deer and bring me safely over the mountains.*

Much depression is caused by trusting in the things of this world instead of in God. We will be disappointed if our happiness is based on security, prestige, possessions, and popularity. These things come and go. Trusting in God helps us travel through the toughest times with surefooted confidence.

What does God think of my struggles?

Psalm 34:18 *The LORD is close to the brokenhearted; he rescues those who are crushed in spirit.*

Psalm 147:3 *He heals the brokenhearted, binding up their wounds.*

Matthew 5:4 *God blesses those who mourn, for they will be comforted.*
God isn't disappointed by our depression and emotional struggles. In fact, we can experience God's presence even more fully in times of brokenness.

Where can I find inspiration and encouragement in times of depression?

Proverbs 16:20 *Those who listen to instruction will prosper; those who trust the LORD will be happy.*

John 15:11 *I have told you this so that you will be filled with my joy. Yes, your joy will overflow!*

When we are depressed, we need to stop listening to the voices of discouragement and listen instead to God's word. The instructions in God's word help us to recognize the lies of the world, the flesh, and the devil that fuel our depression. Trusting the Lord and his word bring us unshakable joy.

Nehemiah 8:10 *Nehemiah continued, "Go and celebrate with a feast of choice foods and sweet drinks, and share gifts of food with people who have nothing prepared. This is a sacred day before our Lord. Don't be dejected and sad, for the joy of the LORD is your strength!"*

2 Corinthians 12:9 *Each time he said, "My gracious favor is all you need. My power works best in your weakness." So now I am glad to boast about my weaknesses, so that the power of Christ may work through me.*
When we are weak we may be more receptive to the Lord's strength. When God works through our weakness we know it is his work and not ours.

Matthew 11:28 *Jesus said, "Come to me, all of you who are weary and carry heavy burdens, and I will give you rest."*
Depression is one of the ways God gets us to rest and to finally slow down long enough to be with the Lord. As we come to him through prayer and the Scriptures, the Holy Spirit comforts and strengthens us—often in ways we cannot explain.

Romans 8:31-32 *What can we say about such wonderful things as these? If God is for us, who can ever be against us? Since God did not spare even his own Son but gave him up for us all, won't God, who gave us Christ, also give us everything else?*
Never underestimate the power of God's affirmation and his willingness to give us all we need for this life. Everything else we need is minimal compared with the infinite and costly gift of Jesus' sacrifice on the cross.

DISAPPOINTMENT

see Depression

DISCERNMENT

When I am confused, where do I turn for clarity, wisdom, understanding, and direction?

James 1:5-8 *If you need wisdom—if you want to know what God wants you to do—ask him, and he will gladly tell you. He will not resent your asking. But when you ask him, be sure that you really expect him to answer, for a doubtful mind is as unsettled as a wave of the sea that is driven and tossed by the wind. People like that should not expect to receive anything from the Lord. They can't make up their minds. They waver back and forth in everything they do.*

Psalm 119:125 *Give discernment to me, your servant; then I will understand your decrees.* Discernment is the ability to interpret events and to understand the true nature of people and situations. Discernment is an aspect of wisdom. It enables us to see behind the facades that mask the truth. Discernment shows us the way through the maze of options that face us. Like the sun that burns away the fog, discernment cuts through confusion and distractions. Whereas the devil is the "father of lies," God is the father of the truth, and he gives discernment to those who seek it.

1 Corinthians 2:12-16 *God has actually given us his Spirit (not the world's spirit) so we can know the wonderful things God has freely given us. When we tell you this, we do not use words of human wisdom. We speak words given to us by the Spirit, using the Spirit's words to explain spiritual truths. But people who aren't Christians can't understand these truths from God's Spirit. It all sounds foolish to them because only those who have the Spirit can understand what the Spirit means. We who have the Spirit understand these things, but others can't understand us at all. How could they? For, "Who can know what the Lord is thinking? Who can give him counsel?" But we can understand these things, for we have the mind of Christ.*

Those who believe in Jesus Christ will find that God gives them a new perspective on life. We have the mind of Christ, coming primarily from God's word. It also comes through the Holy Spirit's guiding our thoughts and decisions.

What are the benefits of discernment?

Proverbs 3:13 *Happy is the person who finds wisdom and gains understanding.*

Proverbs 3:21-23 *My child, don't lose sight of good planning and insight. Hang on to them, for they fill you with life and bring you honor and respect. They keep you safe on your way and keep your feet from stumbling.*

Proverbs 4:12 *If you live a life guided by wisdom, you won't limp or stumble as you run.* Discernment enhances the quality of our life and our discipleship. Godly wisdom and understanding keep us from tripping over the lies and deceptions of the devil.

Proverbs 9:11 *Wisdom will multiply your days and add years to your life.*
Discernment preserves our lives, keeping us from the dangers that threaten to destroy us.

DOUBT

How can I really believe that the Lord cares about me?

Luke 12:6-7 *What is the price of five sparrows? A couple of pennies? Yet God does not forget a single one of them. And the very hairs on your head are all numbered. So don't be afraid; you are more valuable to him than a whole flock of sparrows.*

Psalm 139:13-17 *You made all the delicate, inner parts of my body and knit me together in my mother's womb. Thank you for making me so wonderfully complex! Your workmanship is marvelous—and how well I know it. You watched me as I was being formed in utter seclusion, as I was woven together in the dark of the womb. You saw me before I was born. Every day of my life was recorded in your book. Every moment was laid out before a single day had passed. How precious are your thoughts about me, O God! They are innumerable!*

We think too little of our worth. The Bible assures us time and again that we are God's precious children, the treasures of his eye. God is not so important that he doesn't care about us. He is too great not to care!

What if I find it hard to believe that Jesus Christ was really resurrected?

1 John 1:1-4 *The one who existed from the beginning is the one we have heard and seen. We saw him with our own eyes and touched him with our own hands. He is Jesus Christ, the Word of life. This one who is life from God was shown to us, and we have*

seen him. And now we testify and announce to you that he is the one who is eternal life. He was with the Father, and then he was shown to us. We are telling you about what we ourselves have actually seen and heard, so that you may have fellowship with us. And our fellowship is with the Father and with his Son, Jesus Christ. We are writing these things so that our joy will be complete.

1 Corinthians 15:3-8 *I passed on to you what was most important and what had also been passed on to me—that Christ died for our sins, just as the Scriptures said. He was buried, and he was raised from the dead on the third day, as the Scriptures said. He was seen by Peter and then by the twelve apostles. After that, he was seen by more than five hundred of his followers at one time, most of whom are still alive, though some have died by now. Then he was seen by James and later by all the apostles. Last of all, I saw him, too, long after the others, as though I had been born at the wrong time.* The resurrected Jesus Christ was seen by countless credible witnesses. The disciples were transformed from cringing cowards to courageous witnesses who could not be silenced. The truth of Jesus' claims was validated by his resurrection. If God can bring Christ back from the dead, he can overcome our doubts, too.

How can I trust God when I can't see a way out of my problem?

Genesis 18:13-14 *The LORD said to Abraham, "Why did Sarah laugh? Why did she say, 'Can an old woman like me have a baby?' Is anything too hard for the LORD? About a year from now, just as I told you, I will return, and Sarah will have a son."*

Luke 1:37 *Nothing is impossible with God.* Doubt often arises because we look at the problem instead of looking up to God. God is not limited by our circumstances or by our lack of resources or abilities. Sarah and Abraham, Mary and Joseph, and many other of God's people across the centuries have learned that God can do anything.

Matthew 21:21-22 *Jesus told them, "I assure you, if you have faith and don't doubt, you can do things like this and much more. You can even say to this mountain, 'May God lift you up and throw you into the sea,' and it will happen. If you believe, you will receive whatever you ask for in prayer."*

Luke 12:31-32 *He will give you all you need from day to day if you make the Kingdom of God your primary concern. So don't be afraid, little flock. For it gives your Father great happiness to give you the Kingdom.*

Ephesians 1:14 *The Spirit is God's guarantee that he will give us everything he promised and that he has purchased us to be his own people. This is just one more reason for us to praise our glorious God.*

Hebrews 13:5 *Stay away from the love of money; be satisfied with what you have. For God has said, "I will never fail you. I will never forsake you."*

Romans 10:17 *Faith comes from listening to this message of good news—the Good News about Christ.* When we fill our mind with the promises of God, God fills our lives with the provisions we need. Doubts erode our confidence, but God's promises inspire faith and hope.

Does my doubt keep God from helping me?

Matthew 14:31 *Instantly Jesus reached out his hand and grabbed him. "You don't have much faith," Jesus said. "Why did you doubt me?"*
When Peter was walking on water, he was overcome by doubt. But Jesus did not punish him and allow him to drown. He saved Peter. Doubt can be a starting place for us. We can begin to learn more about our Lord and about our faith. Let your doubts drive you into the word of God and draw you into healthy fellowship with the Lord.

ENCOURAGEMENT

What do I do when I feel overwhelmed?

Leviticus 26:8 *Five of you will chase a hundred, and a hundred of you will chase ten thousand! All your enemies will fall beneath the blows of your weapons.*

Joshua 23:10 *Each one of you will put to flight a thousand of the enemy, for the LORD your God fights for you, just as he has promised.*

Be encouraged that the power of God is for us, regardless of the number of enemies against us. God used David to overcome Goliath, Gideon's three hundred soldiers to defeat the armies of Midian, and one hundred and twenty disciples to establish the church in Acts. He joys when working through our weaknesses and limitations.

Colossians 1:11-14 *We also pray that you will be strengthened with his glorious power so that you will have all the patience and endurance you need. May you be filled with joy, always thanking the Father, who has enabled you to share the inheritance that belongs to God's holy people, who live in the light. For he has rescued us from the one who rules in the kingdom of darkness, and he has brought us into the Kingdom of his dear Son. God has purchased our freedom with his blood and has forgiven all our sins.*

Our encouragement comes from what God has done for us. He has given us the power to be patient and persistent and to keep our minds set on the great hope that awaits us. When we remember that we are already free, the problems of this world lose much of their power over us.

What good can my struggles produce?

2 Corinthians 1:5 *You can be sure that the more we suffer for Christ, the more God will shower us with his comfort through Christ.*
Just as food tastes best when we are hungry, God's comfort is most vivid when we are struggling.

1 Peter 5:10-11 *In his kindness God called you to his eternal glory by means of Jesus Christ. After you have suffered a little while, he will restore, support, and strengthen you, and he will place you on a firm foundation. All power is his forever and ever. Amen.*
Suffering lasts for a brief time, but God's blessing is forever. He not only restores what was lost, but brings new support, strength, and stability to our lives.

ENDURANCE

Where do I find the strength to keep going when I'm tempted to give up?

Galatians 6:9 *Don't get tired of doing what is good. Don't get discouraged and give up, for we will reap a harvest of blessing at the appropriate time.*
Endurance comes from keeping our thoughts on the promise of the harvest, not the problems of the moment.

Philippians 1:6 *I am sure that God, who began the good work within you, will continue his work until it is finally finished on that day when Christ Jesus comes back again.*

Philippians 2:12-13 *Dearest friends, you were always so careful to follow my instructions when I was with you. And now that I am away you must be even more careful to put into action God's saving work in your lives, obeying God with deep reverence and fear. For God is working in you, giving you the desire to obey him and the power to do what pleases him.* We do not endure through our own strength alone. God is at work in our lives. He gives us the strength to keep going when we are exhausted and the reasons to keep believing when we are discouraged.

What purposes do endurance and perseverance serve in my life?

1 Peter 1:6-7 *Be truly glad! There is wonderful joy ahead, even though it is necessary for you to endure many trials for a while. These trials are only to test your faith, to show that it is strong and pure. It is being tested as fire tests and purifies gold—and your faith is far more precious to God than mere gold. So if your faith remains strong after being tried by fiery trials, it will bring you much praise and glory and honor on the day when Jesus Christ is revealed to the whole world.*

2 P e t e r 1 : 5 - 9 *Make every effort to apply the benefits of these promises to your life. Then your faith will produce a life of moral excellence. A life of moral excellence leads to knowing God better. Knowing God leads to self-control. Self-control leads to patient endurance, and patient endurance leads to godliness. Godliness leads to love for other Christians, and finally you will grow to have genuine love for everyone. The more you grow like this, the more you will become productive and useful in your knowledge of our Lord Jesus Christ. But those who fail to develop these virtues are blind or, at least, very shortsighted. They have already forgotten that God has cleansed them from their old life of sin.*

Endurance is like the fire that purifies precious metals and hardens valuable pottery. It cleanses, clarifies, and solidifies our faith. Living through the trials and tests of life is often the most significant way to discover the riches of our faith.

If I already believe in Christ, why do I have to endure?

1 P e t e r 4 : 1 3 *Be very glad—because these trials will make you partners with Christ in his suffering, and afterward you will have the wonderful joy of sharing his glory when it is displayed to all the world.*

H e b r e w s 3 : 1 4 *If we are faithful to the end, trusting God just as firmly as when we first believed, we will share in all that belongs to Christ.*

2 Timothy 2:10-12 *I am willing to endure anything if it will bring salvation and eternal glory in Christ Jesus to those God has chosen. This is a true saying: If we die with him, we will also live with him. If we endure hardship, we will reign with him. If we deny him, he will deny us.*

Matthew 24:13 *Those who endure to the end will be saved.*

Hebrews 10:36 *Patient endurance is what you need now, so you will continue to do God's will. Then you will receive all that he has promised.*

James 1:12 *God blesses the people who patiently endure testing. Afterward they will receive the crown of life that God has promised to those who love him.*

Romans 2:7 *He will give eternal life to those who persist in doing what is good, seeking after the glory and honor and immortality that God offers.* Endurance is an essential quality of Jesus' followers. Though we have the promise of eternal life, we also face the prospect of living in a fallen world out to compromise and destroy our faith. God promises that those who endure will not only survive, but reign with Christ!

1 Peter 2:20 *You get no credit for being patient if you are beaten for doing wrong. But if you suffer for doing right and are patient beneath the blows, God is pleased with you.*

God sees the injustices we suffer. Just as he was pleased with Jesus' submission to the cross, he is pleased when we put his honor above all else.

ENERGY

Why do I sometimes find myself weary and tired?

Isaiah 40:28-31 *Have you never heard or understood? Don't you know that the LORD is the everlasting God, the Creator of all the earth? He never grows faint or weary. No one can measure the depths of his understanding. He gives power to those who are tired and worn out; he offers strength to the weak. Even youths will become exhausted, and young men will give up. But those who wait on the LORD will find new strength. They will fly high on wings like eagles. They will run and not grow weary. They will walk and not faint.*

2 Corinthians 4:7 *This precious treasure—this light and power that now shine within us—is held in perishable containers, that is, in our weak bodies. So everyone can see that our glorious power is from God and is not our own.*

As human beings, we have limitations. We get hungry, tired, and hurt. We are not self-sufficient. Instead of relying on ourselves, we need to rely on the Lord. Like the eagle that soars on the currents of wind, we can trust the Lord to carry us onward.

Where do I turn for energy when I am feeling exhausted?

Matthew 11:28-30 *Jesus said, "Come to me, all of you who are weary and carry heavy burdens, and I will give you rest. Take my yoke upon you. Let me teach you, because I am humble and gentle, and you will find rest for your souls. For my yoke fits perfectly, and the burden I give you is light."*
Jesus invites us to come to him for rest from the weariness of life, strength for the burdens of life, and instruction for the puzzles and problems of life.

Philippians 4:13 *I can do everything with the help of Christ who gives me the strength I need.*
Though we ourselves are limited, we know that Christ provides the power and strength to endure life's hardest trials, most difficult challenges, and toughest obstacles.

How does God expect me to pace my life?

Deuteronomy 5:12-14 *Observe the Sabbath day by keeping it holy, as the LORD your God has commanded you. Six days a week are set apart for your daily duties and regular work, but the seventh day is a day of rest dedicated to the LORD your God. On that day no one in your household may do any kind of work. This includes you, your sons and daughters, your male and female servants, your oxen and donkeys and other livestock, and any foreigners living among you. All your male and female servants must rest as you do.*

Psalm 127:2 *It is useless for you to work so hard from early morning until late at night, anxiously working for food to eat; for God gives rest to his loved ones.*

Jeremiah 31:25 *I have given rest to the weary and joy to the sorrowing.*

A basic source of energy is regular rest. God has designed us to rest daily, weekly, and seasonally. That is why God gave us sleep, the Sabbath, and gave feasts and festivals to ancient Israel. Rest renews us mentally, emotionally, and physically, giving us more energy for the work ahead.

What has God given me as a source of continual energy?

Zechariah 4:6 *He said to me, "This is what the LORD says to Zerubbabel: It is not by force nor by strength, but by my Spirit, says the LORD Almighty."*

Ephesians 3:16 *I pray that from his glorious, unlimited resources he will give you mighty inner strength through his Holy Spirit.*

The Holy Spirit is the indwelling power of God in the believer. When we yield control of our lives to the Lord, he releases his power within us. The Spirit sustains us moment by moment.

Habakkuk 3:19 *The Sovereign LORD is my strength! He will make me as surefooted as a deer and bring me safely over the mountains.*
Even as the deer was created for traveling over difficult terrain with speed and grace, so God's strength empowers us to journey through life's circumstances with grace and power.

EVIL

see also Temptation

Where do I find protection from the threat of evil?

Ephesians 6:10-18 *Be strong with the Lord's mighty power. Put on all of God's armor so that you will be able to stand firm against all strategies and tricks of the Devil. For we are not fighting against people made of flesh and blood, but against the evil rulers and authorities of the unseen world, against those mighty powers of darkness who rule this world, and against wicked spirits in the heavenly realms. Use every piece of God's armor to resist the enemy in the time of evil, so that after the battle you will still be standing firm. Stand your ground, putting on the sturdy belt of truth and the body armor of God's righteousness. For shoes, put on the peace that comes from the Good News, so that you will be fully prepared. In every battle you will need faith as your shield to stop the fiery arrows aimed at you by Satan.*

Put on salvation as your helmet, and take the sword of the Spirit, which is the word of God. Pray at all times and on every occasion in the power of the Holy Spirit. Stay alert and be persistent in your prayers for all Christians everywhere.

This is perhaps the Bible's most comprehensive teaching about the resources believers have to overcome evil. Spiritual forces lurk behind many of our conflicts. Therefore, we should not attack the people manipulated by evil but focus directly on the evil itself. We rely on truth, faith, the power of our testimony, the wisdom of God's word, and the power of prayer. When these are mobilized, evil succumbs, God wins, and we win.

Jude 1:24-25 *All glory to God, who is able to keep you from stumbling, and who will bring you into his glorious presence innocent of sin and with great joy. All glory to him, who alone is God our Savior, through Jesus Christ our Lord. Yes, glory, majesty, power, and authority belong to him, in the beginning, now, and forevermore. Amen.*

Ultimately, it is God's hold on us, not our hold on him, that insures our preservation from evil. That is why we praise and worship him!

How do I confront evil?

Matthew 4:5-7 *The Devil took him to Jerusalem, to the highest point of the Temple, and said, "If you are the Son of God, jump off! For the Scriptures say, 'He orders his angels to protect you. And they will hold you with their hands to keep you from striking your foot on a stone.'" Jesus responded, "The Scriptures also say, 'Do not test the Lord your God.'"*

James 4:7 *Humble yourselves before God. Resist the Devil, and he will flee from you.*

The devil has less power than we think. The devil can tempt us, but he cannot coerce us. He could take Jesus to the top of the temple, but he could not push him off. He can dangle the bait in front of us, but he cannot put the hook in our mouth. We can resist the devil as Jesus did—by responding to the lies of temptation with the truth of God's word.

1 John 4:4 *You belong to God, my dear children. You have already won your fight with these false prophets, because the Spirit who lives in you is greater than the spirit who lives in the world.*

We must never forget that the Holy Spirit is great enough to overcome any threat against us.

What authority do I have when confronting evil?

Romans 8:15-17 *You should not be like cowering, fearful slaves. You should behave instead like God's very own children, adopted into his family—calling him "Father, dear Father." For his Holy Spirit speaks to us deep in our hearts and tells us that we are God's children. And since we are his children, we will share his treasures—for everything God gives to his Son, Christ, is ours, too. But if we are to share his glory, we must also share his suffering.*
One of the tricks of evil is to blind us to our authority and identity as children of God. Through faith in Christ we are children of the King of the universe. Like a crown prince or princess, we can stand tall and firm against any threat against the kingdom.

Matthew 10:1 *Jesus called his twelve disciples to him and gave them authority to cast out evil spirits and to heal every kind of disease and illness.*

Matthew 28:18 *Jesus came and told his disciples, "I have been given complete authority in heaven and on earth."*
Our authority in Christ Jesus not only helps us defend ourselves against temptation and evil, it gives us the power to take the offensive and overcome evil with good.

FAILURE

What is failure in God's eyes?

Colossians 3:23-24 *Work hard and cheerfully at whatever you do, as though you were working for the Lord rather than for people. Remember that the Lord will give you an inheritance as your reward, and the Master you are serving is Christ.*

Often our sense of failure is determined by the level of approval from others. Scripture reminds us to define success in terms of faithfulness to God. God will reward our faithfulness even if we fail in the eyes of the world.

Does failure make God love me less?

Hebrews 2:17-18 *It was necessary for Jesus to be in every respect like us, his brothers and sisters, so that he could be our merciful and faithful High Priest before God. He then could offer a sacrifice that would take away the sins of the people. Since he himself has gone through suffering and temptation, he is able to help us when we are being tempted.*

Hebrews 4:15-16 *This High Priest of ours understands our weaknesses, for he faced all of the same temptations we do, yet he did not sin. So let us come boldly to the throne of our gracious God. There we will receive his mercy, and we will find grace to help us when we need it.*

God loves us unconditionally. Jesus Christ, our High Priest, entered fully into the human experience and knows our trials and temptations. While caring parents may be hurt or saddened by a child's failure, that failure doesn't make them love the child less. In fact, failure often awakens greater tenderness and support toward the child. Just as the Lord understands our weaknesses, our failures help us understand his marvelous grace.

What do I do when I have failed the Lord?

1 Kings 8:33-34 *If your people Israel are defeated by their enemies because they have sinned against you, and if they turn to you and call on your name and pray to you here in this Temple, then hear from heaven and forgive their sins and return them to this land you gave their ancestors.*
Turning to God in repentance and trust is the best response we can have to failure.

1 John 2:1-2 *My dear children, I am writing this to you so that you will not sin. But if you do sin, there is someone to plead for you before the Father. He is Jesus Christ, the one who pleases God completely. He is the sacrifice for our sins. He takes away not only our sins but the sins of all the world.*

Our failure doesn't surprise God. God gave his Son, Jesus Christ, to pay the debt of our failure and bring us back into full fellowship with him. The wonder of the gospel is that our failure revealed God's greatest success.

Lamentations 3:23 *Great is his faithfulness; his mercies begin afresh each day.*
We all long for a clean start, a new slate, a chance to begin again. That's why many people get excited about New Year's resolutions. But every day is a new start in God's mercy. By God's grace and love we are freed from the burden of sin and failure so that we can start afresh.

Hebrews 12:10-11 *Our earthly fathers disciplined us for a few years, doing the best they knew how. But God's discipline is always right and good for us because it means we will share in his holiness. No discipline is enjoyable while it is happening—it is painful! But afterward there will be a quiet harvest of right living for those who are trained in this way.*
Failure doesn't determine our identity or our worth; it is simply feedback on how we are doing. Because God has adopted us as his children, he uses failures to train us, to reveal his love, and to shape us in holiness. Failure is not a dead end—in Christ it becomes the doorway to lasting change.

FAITH

What does faith mean for my everyday life?

Genesis 15:6 *Abram believed the* LORD, *and the* LORD *declared him righteous because of his faith.*

Romans 3:24-25 *Now God in his gracious kindness declares us not guilty. He has done this through Christ Jesus, who has freed us by taking away our sins. For God sent Jesus to take the punishment for our sins and to satisfy God's anger against us. We are made right with God when we believe that Jesus shed his blood, sacrificing his life for us. God was being entirely fair and just when he did not punish those who sinned in former times.*

Faith is our lifeline to God. Sin breaks our relationship with God because a holy God cannot live with unholy people. But when we accept Jesus as Savior and ask him to forgive our sins, our simple act of faith makes us righteous in God's sight.

Isaiah 26:3 *You will keep in perfect peace all who trust in you, whose thoughts are fixed on you!*

Faith in God frees us from the pressures, priorities, and perspectives of this world. It links us to God's peace and power.

How much faith must I have?

Matthew 17:20 *"You didn't have enough faith,"
Jesus told them. "I assure you, even if you had faith as
small as a mustard seed you could say to this
mountain, 'Move from here to there,' and it would
move. Nothing would be impossible."*
The mustard seed was often used to illustrate the
smallest seed known to man. Jesus says that faith
is not a matter of size or quantity. We do not
have to have great faith in God; we have to have
faith in a great God.

How can my faith be strengthened?

Romans 10:17 *Faith comes from listening to this
message of good news—the Good News about Christ.*
Faith is grounded in God's word. It is not simply
a matter of positive thinking or the creation of
human effort. Faith is divinely inspired by the
Holy Spirit working through the word of God.
Our faith grows as we read the stories of God's
work across the centuries and we receive the truth
of his instruction.

John 20:27-29 *He said to Thomas, "Put your
finger here and see my hands. Put your hand into the
wound in my side. Don't be faithless any longer. Believe!"
"My Lord and my God!" Thomas exclaimed. Then Jesus
told him, "You believe because you have seen me. Blessed
are those who haven't seen me and believe anyway."*

The strongest faith is not one based on physical senses but on spiritual conviction. We are not able to be with Jesus in the flesh as were the early disciples, so our faith is strengthened by the testimony of God's word and by the inner conviction of the Holy Spirit.

FAITHFULNESS

How is God faithful to me?

Deuteronomy 7:9 *The LORD your God is indeed God. He is the faithful God who keeps his covenant for a thousand generations and constantly loves those who love him and obey his commands.*

2 Thessalonians 3:3 *The Lord is faithful; he will make you strong and guard you from the evil one.*

Psalm 103:17-18 *The love of the LORD remains forever with those who fear him. His salvation extends to the children's children of those who are faithful to his covenant, of those who obey his commandments!*

Hebrews 13:8 *Jesus Christ is the same yesterday, today, and forever.*

There is nothing more frustrating or more dangerous than an unpredictable, untrustworthy leader. No human on his or her own strength is completely safe, but those who trust in the Lord are perfectly safe. The Lord is not subject to whims or unpredictable mood swings. Our greatest hope is in God's unchanging character and his unwavering love for us. God is perfect in his goodness and grace. We can count on God to remain true to his promises for all eternity.

Why should I be faithful?

Psalm 1:1-3 *Oh, the joys of those who do not follow the advice of the wicked, or stand around with sinners, or join in with scoffers. But they delight in doing everything the LORD wants; day and night they think about his law. They are like trees planted along the riverbank, bearing fruit each season without fail. Their leaves never wither, and in all they do, they prosper.*

The quality of our character affects the quality of our life. Integrity brings continual vitality and bears lasting fruit.

Proverbs 3:3-4 *Never let loyalty and kindness get away from you! Wear them like a necklace; write them deep within your heart. Then you will find favor with both God and people, and you will gain a good reputation.*

One of our greatest securities in life is that of a good name. Faithfulness brings a good reputation and trust from others. When we have problems, sometimes our reputation can be the key to a positive outcome.

2 Timothy 2:11-13 *This is a true saying: If we die with him, we will also live with him. If we endure hardship, we will reign with him. If we deny him, he will deny us. If we are unfaithful, he remains faithful, for he cannot deny himself.*
Faithfulness is not optional. When we fail and fall, we must fall to our knees. Faithfulness is seen not only in our obedience, but also in our repentance.

Hebrews 3:14 *If we are faithful to the end, trusting God just as firmly as when we first believed, we will share in all that belongs to Christ.*

Revelation 2:10 *Don't be afraid of what you are about to suffer. The Devil will throw some of you into prison and put you to the test. You will be persecuted for 'ten days.' Remain faithful even when facing death, and I will give you the crown of life.*
A reward in heaven awaits those who are faithful to God. Faithfulness brings eternal rewards.

Why does faithfulness matter?

Luke 19:17 *"Well done!" the king exclaimed. "You are a trustworthy servant. You have been faithful with the little I entrusted to you, so you will be governor of ten cities as your reward."*

Matthew 24:45-47 *Who is a faithful, sensible servant, to whom the master can give the responsibility of managing his household and feeding his family? If the master returns and finds that the servant has done a good job, there will be a reward. I assure you, the master will put that servant in charge of all he owns.*

1 Corinthians 3:11-15 *No one can lay any other foundation than the one we already have—Jesus Christ. Now anyone who builds on that foundation may use gold, silver, jewels, wood, hay, or straw. But there is going to come a time of testing at the judgment day to see what kind of work each builder has done. Everyone's work will be put through the fire to see whether or not it keeps its value. If the work survives the fire, that builder will receive a reward. But if the work is burned up, the builder will suffer great loss. The builders themselves will be saved, but like someone escaping through a wall of flames.*

The way we live now affects the quality of our life to come. While all who believe in Jesus Christ will inherit eternal life, there will be additional rewards and blessings based on our obedience in this life. Each of us is tested at one point or another. Those who are faithful with what they are given will receive even greater blessings and responsibility.

FAMILY

Does God care about my family?

Psalm 127:1-5 *Unless the LORD builds a house, the work of the builders is useless. Unless the LORD protects a city, guarding it with sentries will do no good. It is useless for you to work so hard from early morning until late at night, anxiously working for food to eat; for God gives rest to his loved ones. Children are a gift from the LORD; they are a reward from him. Children born to a young man are like sharp arrows in a warrior's hands. How happy is the man whose quiver is full of them! He will not be put to shame when he confronts his accusers at the city gates.*
Even as the watchman stood guard over the city while the citizens slept, so the Lord watches over our home so that we can rest securely in him.

Acts 2:38 *Peter replied, "Each of you must turn from your sins and turn to God, and be baptized in the name of Jesus Christ for the forgiveness of your sins. Then you will receive the gift of the Holy Spirit."*

Isaiah 59:21 *"This is my covenant with them," says the LORD. "My Spirit will not leave them, and neither will these words I have given you. They will be on your lips and on the lips of your children and your children's children forever. I, the LORD, have spoken!"*

Too often we think of our relationship with God in individualistic terms. God cares about families, too. We can pray for our families and for future generations, knowing that God wants to redeem them and care for them.

How can I best care for my family?

Proverbs 22:6 *Teach your children to choose the right path, and when they are older, they will remain upon it.*

Proverbs 6:20-23 *My son, obey your father's commands, and don't neglect your mother's teaching. Keep their words always in your heart. Tie them around your neck. Wherever you walk, their counsel can lead you. When you sleep, they will protect you. When you wake up in the morning, they will advise you. For these commands and this teaching are a lamp to light the way ahead of you. The correction of discipline is the way to life.*

God's promises of protection are supported by our commitment to obedience. When our families develop a real appreciation for God's truth and wisdom for living, they have the greatest tools for effective living.

Ephesians 6:1-4 *Children, obey your parents because you belong to the Lord, for this is the right thing to do. "Honor your father and mother." This is the first of the Ten Commandments that ends with a promise. And this is the promise: If you honor your father and mother, "you will live a long life, full of blessing." And now a word to you fathers. Don't make your children angry by the way you treat them. Rather, bring them up with the discipline and instruction approved by the Lord.*

Honoring our families is one of the pathways to receiving God's promises. Parents are entrusted to teach their children to walk in God's ways and to discipline in love. Children are to respond with respect and obedience. When these happen, good things follow.

What will God do for my family?

Psalm 112:1-3 *Praise the LORD! Happy are those who fear the LORD. Yes, happy are those who delight in doing what he commands. Their children will be successful everywhere; an entire generation of godly people will be blessed. They themselves will be wealthy, and their good deeds will never be forgotten.*

Proverbs 20:7 *The godly walk with integrity; blessed are their children after them.*

The Lord is so gracious that he not only blesses us, but also blesses those we most love. We can trust our families into his everlasting care.

FEAR

see also Courage

What can I do when I am overcome with fear? How do I find the strength to go on?

Psalm 46:1-2 *God is our refuge and strength, always ready to help in times of trouble. So we will not fear, even if earthquakes come and the mountains crumble into the sea.*

John 14:27 *I am leaving you with a gift—peace of mind and heart. And the peace I give isn't like the peace the world gives. So don't be troubled or afraid.*
God is greater than the most severe threats in life. We will not be surprised or overcome by trouble if we continually turn to the Lord.

2 Timothy 1:7 *God has not given us a spirit of fear and timidity, but of power, love, and self-discipline.*
Debilitating fear is not from the Lord. We can call upon God's Spirit to give us the power to face our foes, the love to overcome evil with good, and the discipline to persevere through our trials. We have been given the power to turn from fear to faith.

How can I confront the sources of my fear?

Psalm 27:1-3 *The LORD is my light and my salvation—so why should I be afraid? The LORD protects me from danger—so why should I tremble? When evil people come to destroy me, when my enemies and foes attack me, they will stumble and fall. Though a mighty army surrounds me, my heart will know no fear. Even if they attack me, I remain confident.*

Romans 8:31-32 *What can we say about such wonderful things as these? If God is for us, who can ever be against us? Since God did not spare even his own Son but gave him up for us all, won't God, who gave us Christ, also give us everything else?*

Fear can come from human intimidation, fueled by irrational anxiety. Both the psalmist and Paul remind us to look not at the mortal creatures who threaten us, but at the Lord God Almighty who loves us. God is for us. Instead of fearing others, we can face them with courage and confidence because we know their limitations. We also know our enemies will ultimately answer to God.

Isaiah 41:10 *Don't be afraid, for I am with you. Do not be dismayed, for I am your God. I will strengthen you. I will help you. I will uphold you with my victorious right hand.*

God's presence calms our panic. God's care is the antidote to our despair. God's power resolves our problems.

How does God deal with threats against me?

Psalm 91:1-7, 11 *Those who live in the shelter of the Most High will find rest in the shadow of the Almighty. This I declare of the LORD: He alone is my refuge, my place of safety; he is my God, and I am trusting him. For he will rescue you from every trap and protect you from the fatal plague. He will shield you with his wings. He will shelter you with his feathers. His faithful promises are your armor and protection. Do not be afraid of the terrors of the night, nor fear the dangers of the day, nor dread the plague that stalks in darkness, nor the disaster that strikes at midday. Though a thousand fall at your side, though ten thousand are dying around you, these evils will not touch you. . . . He orders his angels to protect you wherever you go.*

This passage of Scripture has been a constant source of courage and encouragement throughout the centuries. It reminds us that while the threats in this world are seemingly endless, the promise of God's protection is infinitely greater.

Luke 12:11-12 *When you are brought to trial in the synagogues and before rulers and authorities, don't worry about what to say in your defense, for the Holy Spirit will teach you what needs to be said even as you are standing there.*

When we are faithful, we will sometimes find ourselves in very tough situations. Even then we can call upon the Lord for the courage to speak the truth confidently, and he will give the words.

FELLOWSHIP

How does the Lord change the quality of our fellowship?

Matthew 18:20 *Where two or three gather together because they are mine, I am there among them.*

The promise of the Lord's presence transforms our fellowship. We draw strength from the testimony of God's faithfulness in others' lives. We learn to comfort one another with the comfort we receive from the Lord. And we experience love and forgiveness in practical ways.

How does God provide for us through fellowship?

Acts 4:32-35 *All the believers were of one heart and mind, and they felt that what they owned was not their own; they shared everything they had. And the apostles gave powerful witness to the resurrection of the Lord Jesus, and God's great favor was upon them all. There was no poverty among them, because people who owned land or houses sold them and brought the money to the apostles to give to others in need.*

Our fellowship with other believers is meant to provide for our needs in the most practical ways. God's love for us moves us to share our resources with each other. This practical expression of love unleashes God's power and empowers our witness to the world.

What does God promise when we make healthy fellowship a priority?

1 John 1:5-7 *This is the message he has given us to announce to you: God is light and there is no darkness in him at all. So we are lying if we say we have fellowship with God but go on living in spiritual darkness. We are not living in the truth. But if we are living in the light of God's presence, just as Christ is, then we have fellowship with each other, and the blood of Jesus, his Son, cleanses us from every sin.* We ignore godly fellowship at great peril, for God rewards godly fellowship with great blessing. We often experience God more fully when we live in open relationship with each other.

1 Peter 3:8-9 *All of you should be of one mind, full of sympathy toward each other, loving one another with tender hearts and humble minds. Don't repay evil for evil. Don't retaliate when people say unkind things about you. Instead, pay them back with a blessing. That is what God wants you to do, and he will bless you for it.*

Psalm 34:12-15 *Do any of you want to live a life that is long and good? Then watch your tongue! Keep your lips from telling lies! Turn away from evil and do good. Work hard at living in peace with others. The eyes of the LORD watch over those who do right; his ears are open to their cries for help.*

Our spiritual well-being depends on the quality of our relationships. God promises to watch out for us as we watch out for those he loves.

FORGIVENESS

What can I do if I feel guilty?

1 John 1:8-9 *If we say we have no sin, we are only fooling ourselves and refusing to accept the truth. But if we confess our sins to him, he is faithful and just to forgive us and to cleanse us from every wrong.*

Acts 2:38 *Each of you must turn from your sins and turn to God, and be baptized in the name of Jesus Christ for the forgiveness of your sins. Then you will receive the gift of the Holy Spirit.*

We receive God's forgiveness when we confess our sins to him. To confess means to agree with God that we have done wrong. Through Jesus Christ, God accepts our confession and forgives us. There is nothing more we must do. We must not let lingering feelings of shame persuade us otherwise.

Matthew 26:28 *This is my blood, which seals the covenant between God and his people. It is poured out to forgive the sins of many.*
Jesus gave his life so that we could be forgiven and reconciled to God. When we put our trust in him, he pays our debt in full.

2 Chronicles 7:14 *If my people who are called by my name will humble themselves and pray and seek my face and turn from their wicked ways, I will hear from heaven and will forgive their sins and heal their land.*

Psalm 51:17 *The sacrifice you want is a broken spirit. A broken and repentant heart, O God, you will not despise.*
God is more ready to forgive than we are to repent. A broken spirit is the quickest way to spiritual wholeness.

What happens when I confess my sin?

Romans 8:1 *Now there is no condemnation for those who belong to Christ Jesus.*
The amazing truth of the gospel is that those who trust in Jesus Christ for forgiveness are forever free from God's judgment. That makes us more grateful and more eager to honor the Lord by godly living.

Psalm 103:3, 10-12 *He forgives all my sins and heals all my diseases. . . . He has not punished us for all our sins, nor does he deal with us as we deserve. For his unfailing love toward those who fear him is as great as the height of the heavens above the earth. He has removed our rebellious acts as far away from us as the east is from the west.*

Isaiah 43:25 *I—yes, I alone—am the one who blots out your sins for my own sake and will never think of them again.*

When we confess our sins and trust Jesus Christ, our sins are wiped away. They will not be held against us. We are freely and fully pardoned by the Lord and should forgive ourselves as well.

Can any sin be forgiven?

Joel 2:32 *Anyone who calls on the name of the LORD will be saved. There will be people on Mount Zion in Jerusalem who escape, just as the LORD has said. These will be among the survivors whom the LORD has called.*

Mark 3:28-29 *I assure you that any sin can be forgiven, including blasphemy; but anyone who blasphemes against the Holy Spirit will never be forgiven. It is an eternal sin.*

Romans 8:38 *I am convinced that nothing can ever separate us from his love. Death can't, and life can't. The angels can't, and the demons can't. Our fears for today, our worries about tomorrow, and even the powers of hell can't keep God's love away.*
Forgiveness is not based on the magnitude of the sin, but the magnitude of the forgiver's love. No sin is too great for God's complete and unconditional love. The Bible does, however, mention one unforgivable sin—harboring an attitude of defiant hostility toward God that prevents us from accepting his forgiveness. Those who don't want his forgiveness place themselves out of its reach.

Isaiah 1:18 *"Come now, let us argue this out,"* says the LORD. *"No matter how deep the stain of your sins, I can remove it. I can make you as clean as freshly fallen snow. Even if you are stained as red as crimson, I can make you as white as wool."*
Forgiveness means that God looks at us as though we never sinned. We are blameless before him.

Do I have to forgive others who hurt me?

Matthew 6:14-15 *If you forgive those who sin against you, your heavenly Father will forgive you. But if you refuse to forgive others, your Father will not forgive your sins.*
We will receive God's forgiveness only when we are willing to forgive others. Being unwilling to forgive shows that we have not understood or benefitted from God's forgiveness.

Luke 17:3-4 *I am warning you! If another believer sins, rebuke him; then if he repents, forgive him. Even if he wrongs you seven times a day and each time turns again and asks forgiveness, forgive him.*

Matthew 18:21-22 *Peter came to him and asked, "Lord, how often should I forgive someone who sins against me? Seven times?" "No!" Jesus replied, "seventy times seven!"*

Just as God forgives us without limit, we should forgive others without keeping score.

Luke 23:34 *Jesus said, "Father, forgive these people, because they don't know what they are doing." And the soldiers gambled for his clothes by throwing dice.*

Jesus forgave those who mocked and killed him.

Colossians 3:13 *You must make allowance for each other's faults and forgive the person who offends you. Remember, the Lord forgave you, so you must forgive others.*

1 Peter 3:8-9 *All of you should be of one mind, full of sympathy toward each other, loving one another with tender hearts and humble minds. Don't repay evil for evil. Don't retaliate when people say unkind things about you. Instead, pay them back with a blessing. That is what God wants you to do, and he will bless you for it.*

God wants us to respond to others' sins against us by blessing them.

FRIENDSHIP

see Fellowship

FUTURE

see also Guidance, Heaven

What do I have to look forward to?

1 Peter 1:4-5 *God has reserved a priceless inheritance for his children. It is kept in heaven for you, pure and undefiled, beyond the reach of change and decay. And God, in his mighty power, will protect you until you receive this salvation, because you are trusting him. It will be revealed on the last day for all to see.*

We who are God's children will inherit the heavenly riches reserved for us. Until we enter heaven, God preserves our inheritance and protects us.

1 Corinthians 2:9-10 *The Scriptures . . . say, "No eye has seen, no ear has heard, and no mind has imagined what God has prepared for those who love him." But we know these things because God has revealed them to us by his Spirit, and his Spirit searches out everything and shows us even God's deep secrets.*

We who love God have a glorious future ahead, beyond our present understanding.

1 Corinthians 15:54-58 *When this happens—when our perishable earthly bodies have been transformed into heavenly bodies that will never die—then at last the Scriptures will come true: "Death is swallowed up in victory. O death, where is your victory? O death, where is your sting?" For sin is the sting that results in death, and the law gives sin its power. How we thank God, who gives us victory over sin and death through Jesus Christ our Lord! So, my dear brothers and sisters, be strong and steady, always enthusiastic about the Lord's work, for you know that nothing you do for the Lord is ever useless.* Those who trust Jesus Christ need have no fear as they face death. Death is simply a doorway into our heavenly home. This hope of eternal life gives us courage and discipline for life now. We know that nothing we do for the Lord will be wasted or forgotten.

How can I be sure God will direct my future in this life?

Psalm 32:8 *The LORD says, "I will guide you along the best pathway for your life. I will advise you and watch over you."*
The Lord directs our steps. Though the pathway may lead through dark valleys or seem to take unnecessary detours, we will one day look back and discover that the Lord's way was best.

Jeremiah 29:11 *"I know the plans I have for you," says the LORD. "They are plans for good and not for disaster, to give you a future and a hope."*
Too often we doubt God's care. We are tempted to think he is neglecting us or giving us the bare minimum. We have hope in the knowledge that God, our loving Creator, will always give us his best.

Philippians 1:6 *I am sure that God, who began the good work within you, will continue his work until it is finally finished on that day when Christ Jesus comes back again.*
God finishes what he starts. We should not allow the limitations of our finite perspective to blind us to the promise that God will complete his work in us. Our future is secure in Christ.

How can hope for the future help me live today?

Romans 8:18-25 *What we suffer now is nothing compared to the glory he will give us later. For all creation is waiting eagerly for that future day when God will reveal who his children really are. Against its will, everything on earth was subjected to God's curse. All creation anticipates the day when it will join God's children in glorious freedom from death and decay. For we know that all creation has been groaning as in the pains of childbirth right up to the present time. And even we Christians, although we have the Holy Spirit within us as a foretaste of future glory, also groan to be released from pain and suffering. We, too, wait anxiously for that day when God will give us our full rights as his children, including the new bodies he has promised us. Now that we are saved, we eagerly look forward to this freedom. For if you already have something, you don't need to hope for it. But if we look forward to something we don't have yet, we must wait patiently and confidently.*

We have strength and courage to face the trials and suffering of this life because we can look beyond them to the glory that God has in store for us.

Matthew 19:29 *Everyone who has given up houses or brothers or sisters or father or mother or children or property, for my sake, will receive a hundred times as much in return and will have eternal life.*

We know that sacrifices we make now will be rewarded by God.

GIVING

see also Money, Tithing

How does giving to others affect my own life?

Acts 20:35 *I have been a constant example of how you can help the poor by working hard. You should remember the words of the Lord Jesus: "It is more blessed to give than to receive."*

Keeping something may please us, but giving gives us the joy of pleasing God and the satisfaction of helping others.

Luke 6:38 *If you give, you will receive. Your gift will return to you in full measure, pressed down, shaken together to make room for more, and running over. Whatever measure you use in giving—large or small—it will be used to measure what is given back to you.*

We cannot outgive God. While we should not give in order to get, God has promised to bless us in response to our giving. Those who trust him find that they always have what they need when they really need it.

Psalm 112:5-6 *All goes well for those who are generous, who lend freely and conduct their business fairly. Such people will not be overcome by evil circumstances. Those who are righteous will be long remembered.*

God blesses the generous with things that money can never buy.

Matthew 10:42 *If you give even a cup of cold water to one of the least of my followers, you will surely be rewarded.*

The simplest gifts bring the most sacred rewards. No gift is too small, and no act of kindness is too insignificant to go unnoticed by the Lord.

What if I don't seem to have enough to give?

Proverbs 3:9-10 *Honor the LORD with your wealth and with the best part of everything your land produces. Then he will fill your barns with grain, and your vats will overflow with the finest wine.*

2 Corinthians 9:8 *God will generously provide all you need. Then you will always have everything you need and plenty left over to share with others.*

Proverbs 28:27 *Whoever gives to the poor will lack nothing. But a curse will come upon those who close their eyes to poverty.*

Ecclesiastes 11:1 *Give generously, for your gifts will return to you later.*

God promises to provide for us as we give to others.

GODLINESS

see Holy/Holiness, Temptation

GRACE

see also Forgiveness

What is grace?

Romans 6:23 *The wages of sin is death, but the free gift of God is eternal life through Christ Jesus our Lord.*

When the Bible says we are saved by grace, it means that God has freely chosen to pardon our sin through Jesus Christ. We do not have to earn God's love or work our way to heaven. By grace, we are forgiven for our sin and restored to full fellowship with God.

Ephesians 2:8-9 *God saved you by his special favor when you believed. And you can't take credit for this; it is a gift from God. Salvation is not a reward for the good things we have done, so none of us can boast about it.*

Grace is God's special favor. Like the gift of life itself, we cannot take credit for it any more than a baby can brag about being born! The fact that this is God's gift and not the product of our own effort gives us great comfort, security, and hope.

How does grace affect my daily life?

Romans 6:14 *Sin is no longer your master, for you are no longer subject to the law, which enslaves you to sin. Instead, you are free by God's grace.*

God's grace forgives the penalty of sin and breaks the power of sin in our daily lives. The Holy Spirit renews our will, and the word of God renews our minds so that we are able to discern truth and follow God's ways.

How does grace affect my view of God?

Psalm 103:8 *The LORD is merciful and gracious; he is slow to get angry and full of unfailing love.* What we believe about God is the most important thing about us. If we believe that God is always angry, we will be defensive, fearful, or antagonistic toward God. When we believe the depth of his love and grace toward us, we enter into joy and freedom.

GRIEF

see Comfort, Death/Dying

GUIDANCE

see also Will of God

How can I be sure God will guide me?

Psalm 32:8 *The LORD says, "I will guide you along the best pathway for your life. I will advise you and watch over you."*

Psalm 37:23-24 *The steps of the godly are directed by the LORD. He delights in every detail of their lives. Though they stumble, they will not fall, for the LORD holds them by the hand.*

Luke 12:6-7 *What is the price of five sparrows? A couple of pennies? Yet God does not forget a single one of them. And the very hairs on your head are all*

*numbered. So don't be afraid; you are more valuable
to him than a whole flock of sparrows.*
Jesus gives this promise to all his followers: If
God values the littlest things of his creation, how
much more must he value us for whom he gave
his own precious Son. When we are anxious or
concerned, we need to remind ourselves that God
does indeed care about us and is watching over
us.

Jeremiah 29:11 *"I know the plans I have for
you," says the LORD. "They are plans for good and not
for disaster, to give you a future and a hope."*
God is always seeking the best future for us. There
are times that we delay it through our
disobedience, but when we come back to God, he
is always ready to give us his best.

How can I experience God's guidance?

Proverbs 3:5-6 *Trust in the LORD with all your
heart; do not depend on your own understanding.
Seek his will in all you do, and he will direct your
paths.*
The first step in guidance is knowing where to put
your trust. Travelers rely on maps when visiting
new places. In the same way, we must trust God
to lead us and realize our own limitations. We do
not understand all the complexities of life, but
the Lord does.

Matthew 7:7-11 *Keep on asking, and you will be given what you ask for. Keep on looking, and you will find. Keep on knocking, and the door will be opened. For everyone who asks, receives. Everyone who seeks, finds. And the door is opened to everyone who knocks. You parents—if your children ask for a loaf of bread, do you give them a stone instead? Or if they ask for a fish, do you give them a snake? Of course not! If you sinful people know how to give good gifts to your children, how much more will your heavenly Father give good gifts to those who ask him.*

God invites us to pray so that we will know him more fully as our loving Father and understand ourselves more clearly as well. Even as a parent gives more and more responsibility to a child as he or she grows, so the Lord expects us to take responsibility for seeking and following his direction.

GUILT

see also Forgiveness

What can I do to be free from my guilt?

Romans 3:20-26 *No one can ever be made right in God's sight by doing what his law commands. For the more we know God's law, the clearer it becomes that we aren't obeying it. But now God has shown us a different way of being right in his sight—not by obeying the law but by the way promised in the*

Scriptures long ago. We are made right in God's sight when we trust in Jesus Christ to take away our sins. And we all can be saved in this same way, no matter who we are or what we have done. For all have sinned; all fall short of God's glorious standard. Yet now God in his gracious kindness declares us not guilty. He has done this through Christ Jesus, who has freed us by taking away our sins. For God sent Jesus to take the punishment for our sins and to satisfy God's anger against us. We are made right with God when we believe that Jesus shed his blood, sacrificing his life for us. God was being entirely fair and just when he did not punish those who sinned in former times. And he is entirely fair and just in this present time when he declares sinners to be right in his sight because they believe in Jesus.

This is the gospel in a nutshell: God knows we are guilty and knows we cannot save ourselves. He has done for us what we cannot do for ourselves. He sent Jesus Christ to pay the penalty for our sin. When we trust in him, the consequence of our sin is fully removed.

How do I handle lingering guilt feelings, even after I have confessed my sin?

A c t s   1 3 : 3 9   *Everyone who believes in him is freed from all guilt and declared right with God— something the Jewish law could never do.*

1   J o h n   1 : 9   *If we confess our sins to him, he is*

faithful and just to forgive us and to cleanse us from every wrong.

Psalm 51:7 *Purify me from my sins, and I will be clean; wash me, and I will be whiter than snow.*
Sometimes it is hard to believe the Good News. We need to trust God's truth, not our fickle, fluctuating feelings. Most of our guilt is really shame and regret over what we have done. Along with confessing our sins, we need to claim God's promise to cleanse us from shame and regret as well.

HABITS

see also Addiction

How can God help me deal with bad habits?

Romans 8:5-6 *Those who are dominated by the sinful nature think about sinful things, but those who are controlled by the Holy Spirit think about things that please the Spirit. If your sinful nature controls your mind, there is death. But if the Holy Spirit controls your mind, there is life and peace.*
God has given us the Holy Spirit to help make us holy. While victory does not come immediately, we will progress as we fill our minds and hearts with spiritual truth and the promises of God.

Romans 6:12-14 *Do not let sin control the way*

*you live; do not give in to its lustful desires. Do not let
any part of your body become a tool of wickedness, to
be used for sinning. Instead, give yourselves
completely to God since you have been given new life.
And use your whole body as a tool to do what is right
for the glory of God. Sin is no longer your master, for
you are no longer subject to the law, which enslaves
you to sin. Instead, you are free by God's grace.*
One of Satan's great lies is that we are victims
who have no power to resist sin. The world
teaches us that heredity, environment, and
circumstance excuse us from responsibility. But
God is more powerful than anything that seeks to
control us. When we call upon his power through
prayer and the support of fellow believers, God
breaks our chains and sets us free.

How can God help me cultivate good habits?

1 Timothy 4:7-8 *Do not waste time arguing
over godless ideas and old wives' tales. Spend your
time and energy in training yourself for spiritual
fitness. Physical exercise has some value, but spiritual
exercise is much more important, for it promises a
reward in both this life and the next.*

1 Corinthians 9:25 *All athletes practice strict
self-control. They do it to win a prize that will fade
away, but we do it for an eternal prize.*
Godly habits—such as reading the Bible, praying,

115

and giving our time and money in service—give us spiritual stamina, purpose, and direction for our lives. They also help us keep our eyes on the eternal prize.

HAPPINESS

see Joy

HEALING

Does God heal us?

Exodus 15:26 *If you will listen carefully to the voice of the LORD your God and do what is right in his sight, obeying his commands and laws, then I will not make you suffer the diseases I sent on the Egyptians; for I am the LORD who heals you.*
God is not bound by the limitations of this world. He can overcome any threat in our lives—physical, mental, spiritual, or emotional.

Luke 5:12-13 *In one of the villages, Jesus met a man with an advanced case of leprosy. When the man saw Jesus, he fell to the ground, face down in the dust, begging to be healed. "Lord," he said, "if you want to, you can make me well again." Jesus reached out and touched the man. "I want to," he said. "Be healed!" And instantly the leprosy disappeared.*

Jesus has the ability and the willingness to heal us. We are not bothering God when we pray for healing; we are expressing our faith and trust in him.

Psalm 147:3 *He heals the brokenhearted, binding up their wounds.*

Malachi 4:2 *For you who fear my name, the Sun of Righteousness will rise with healing in his wings. And you will go free, leaping with joy like calves let out to pasture.*
God's healing can reach every level of our lives. His healing brings a joy and freedom that cannot be contained.

How can I seek God's healing?

James 5:13-16 *Are any among you suffering? They should keep on praying about it. And those who have reason to be thankful should continually sing praises to the Lord. Are any among you sick? They should call for the elders of the church and have them pray over them, anointing them with oil in the name of the Lord. And their prayer offered in faith will heal the sick, and the Lord will make them well. And anyone who has committed sins will be forgiven. Confess your sins to each other and pray for each other so that you may be healed. The earnest prayer of a righteous person has great power and wonderful results.*

The Lord often uses others to give us his gifts—including healing. He has given authority to church leaders to be vessels for this special work. While we may not feel worthy or capable, we should pray for one another in obedience to God's direction.

Psalm 32:3-5 *When I refused to confess my sin, I was weak and miserable, and I groaned all day long. Day and night your hand of discipline was heavy on me. My strength evaporated like water in the summer heat. Finally, I confessed all my sins to you and stopped trying to hide them. I said to myself, "I will confess my rebellion to the LORD." And you forgave me! All my guilt is gone.*

Psalm 103:3 *He forgives all my sins and heals all my diseases.*
Sin can make us sick, literally. Healing can come if we repent of our sin and receive God's forgiveness.

Psalm 119:93 *I will never forget your commandments, for you have used them to restore my joy and health.*
Following God's direction can bring healing in our lives. God's word shows us how to break free from the stress, the pressure, and the unhealthy practices that undermine our health.

What if God doesn't heal me, or one I care about, physically?

Psalm 73:24-26 *You will keep on guiding me with your counsel, leading me to a glorious destiny. Whom have I in heaven but you? I desire you more than anything on earth. My health may fail, and my spirit may grow weak, but God remains the strength of my heart; he is mine forever.*

Whether or not God chooses to heal us physically, we can have the unspeakable gift of knowing the him personally. His love and the promise of eternal life with him are our greatest sources of comfort and hope.

HEALTH

see Healing

HEAVEN

Is there really a heaven?

Ecclesiastes 3:11 *God has made everything beautiful for its own time. He has planted eternity in the human heart, but even so, people cannot see the whole scope of God's work from beginning to end.*

God created us with an instinct for heaven, an inner longing to live forever. It is not just wishful thinking; it is God's intended purpose for us.

John 14:2 *There are many rooms in my Father's home, and I am going to prepare a place for you. If this were not so, I would tell you plainly.*

2 Corinthians 5:1 *For we know that when this earthly tent we live in is taken down—when we die and leave these bodies—we will have a home in heaven, an eternal body made for us by God himself and not by human hands.*

Heaven is described most often in terms of being our home. It is not a paradise we will simply visit on vacation, but an eternal dwelling place where we will live in joyful fellowship with our heavenly Father and his family.

1 Corinthians 15:20 *Christ has been raised from the dead. He has become the first of a great harvest of those who will be raised to life again.*

Jesus' resurrection gives us the promise and assurance of our own resurrection to heaven and of eternal life.

Revelation 21:3-4 *I heard a loud shout from the throne, saying, "Look, the home of God is now among his people! He will live with them, and they will be his people. God himself will be with them. He will remove all of their sorrows, and there will be no more death or sorrow or crying or pain. For the old world and its evils are gone forever."*

The promise of Scripture is that God will remove all the sin and struggles of this fallen world and create a new heaven and new earth. The best this world has to offer can't even compare with the glory to come!

How can I be certain I will go to heaven?

Hebrews 2:14-15 *Because God's children are human beings—made of flesh and blood—Jesus also became flesh and blood by being born in human form. For only as a human being could he die, and only by dying could he break the power of the Devil, who had the power of death. Only in this way could he deliver those who have lived all their lives as slaves to the fear of dying.*

Apart from Jesus Christ, death is a terrifying destiny—it is God's judgment against sin. But Jesus Christ has broken the power of death and overcome the fear of death for those who have faith in him.

John 3:16 *God so loved the world that he gave his only Son, so that everyone who believes in him will not perish but have eternal life.*

John 14:6 *Jesus told him, "I am the way, the truth, and the life. No one can come to the Father except through me.*

Trusting Jesus Christ is the only way to heaven. When we trust in him, we need have no doubt whatsoever. God is faithful and will keep his promise.

Romans 8:35-39 *Can anything ever separate us from Christ's love? Does it mean he no longer loves us if we have trouble or calamity, or are persecuted, or are hungry or cold or in danger or threatened with death? (Even the Scriptures say, "For your sake we are killed every day; we are being slaughtered like sheep.") No, despite all these things, overwhelming victory is ours through Christ, who loved us. And I am convinced that nothing can ever separate us from his love. Death can't, and life can't. The angels can't, and the demons can't. Our fears for today, our worries about tomorrow, and even the powers of hell can't keep God's love away. Whether we are high above the sky or in the deepest ocean, nothing in all creation will ever be able to separate us from the love of God that is revealed in Christ Jesus our Lord.* God's love is stronger than any person, supernatural foe, or circumstance that may threaten us. No matter what comes our way, nothing can separate us from God's love when we trust in Jesus Christ.

HELP

see Rescue

HOLY/HOLINESS

see also Temptation

How is it possible for me to be holy?

Leviticus 21:8 *You must treat them as holy because they offer up food to your God. You must consider them holy because I, the LORD, am holy, and I make you holy.*

God is the only one who can make us holy. The word *holy* comes from the root word which means "to be separate or set apart." As such, holiness includes not only moral integrity, but an entirely different outlook on life—as we realize that we are in the world, but not of it. God promises to help us break free from the attractions of this world so that we can live for him.

Ephesians 1:4 *Long ago, even before he made the world, God loved us and chose us in Christ to be holy and without fault in his eyes.*

Ephesians 5:25-27 *You husbands must love your wives with the same love Christ showed the church. He gave up his life for her to make her holy and clean, washed by baptism and God's word. He did this to present her to himself as a glorious church without a spot or wrinkle or any other blemish. Instead, she will be holy and without fault.*

1 Corinthians 1:30 *God alone made it possible for you to be in Christ Jesus. For our benefit God made Christ to be wisdom itself. He is the one who made us acceptable to God. He made us pure and holy, and he gave himself to purchase our freedom.*

We are brought into a state of holiness not by what we do, but by what Jesus did for us, cleansing and forgiving us from sin.

How can my life become more holy?

Romans 12:1-2 *Dear brothers and sisters, I plead with you to give your bodies to God. Let them be a living and holy sacrifice—the kind he will accept. When you think of what he has done for you, is this too much to ask? Don't copy the behavior and customs of this world, but let God transform you into a new person by changing the way you think. Then you will know what God wants you to do, and you will know how good and pleasing and perfect his will really is.*
The Lord changes our lives from the inside out. He renews our minds. When we yield to his control, the great questions of life are answered. We learn what God wants us to do and are able to live as God wants us to live.

Acts 20:32 *Now I entrust you to God and the word of his grace—his message that is able to build you up and give you an inheritance with all those he has set apart for himself.*

John 17:17 *Make them pure and holy by teaching them your words of truth.*
Jesus' prayer for us assures us that God will do everything possible to bring us to holiness. God's word both instructs and inspires us to become holy and mature in our faith.

How does God reward those who seek holiness?

Psalm 112:1-4, 6-8 *Praise the LORD! Happy are those who fear the LORD. Yes, happy are those who delight in doing what he commands. Their children will be successful everywhere; an entire generation of godly people will be blessed. They themselves will be wealthy, and their good deeds will never be forgotten. When darkness overtakes the godly, light will come bursting in. They are generous, compassionate, and righteous. . . . Such people will not be overcome by evil circumstances. Those who are righteous will be long remembered. They do not fear bad news; they confidently trust the LORD to care for them. They are confident and fearless and can face their foes triumphantly.*

Holy living has countless practical benefits. It brings peace to our lives. More importantly, holiness gives us close fellowship with the God we love.

HOLY SPIRIT

When do I receive the Holy Spirit?

Ephesians 1:13-14 *Now you also have heard the truth, the Good News that God saves you. And when you believed in Christ, he identified you as his own by giving you the Holy Spirit, whom he promised long ago. The Spirit is God's guarantee that he will give us everything he promised and that he has purchased us to be his own people. This is just one more reason for us to praise our glorious God.*

God gives us the Holy Spirit when we believe in Jesus Christ. Some would even say that God gives us the Holy Spirit to enable us to believe in Christ.

Ezekiel 36:25-27 *I will sprinkle clean water on you, and you will be clean. Your filth will be washed away, and you will no longer worship idols. And I will give you a new heart with new and right desires, and I will put a new spirit in you. I will take out your stony heart of sin and give you a new, obedient heart. And I will put my Spirit in you so you will obey my laws and do whatever I command.*

Acts 2:16-18 *What you see this morning was predicted centuries ago by the prophet Joel: "In the last days, God said, I will pour out my Spirit upon all people. Your sons and daughters will prophesy, your young men will see visions, and your old men will dream dreams. In those days I will pour out my Spirit upon all my servants, men and women alike, and they will prophesy."*

The gift of the Holy Spirit was promised long ago, but was not finally given until Jesus Christ was resurrected and ascended into heaven. Peter's preaching at Pentecost marked the dramatic outpouring of the Spirit, fulfilling the prophecies of old.

Luke 11:11-13 *You fathers—if your children ask for a fish, do you give them a snake instead? Or if they ask for an egg, do you give them a scorpion? Of course not! If you sinful people know how to give good gifts to your children, how much more will your heavenly Father give the Holy Spirit to those who ask him.*
Though the Holy Spirit lives within us, we pray expectantly that God will release more and more of the Spirit's power in our lives. In a way, the Holy Spirit is like the potential power of a dammed up reservoir of water—only when it flows through the turbines will it generate the power we need.

Luke 12:11-12 *When you are brought to trial in the synagogues and before rulers and authorities, don't worry about what to say in your defense, for the Holy Spirit will teach you what needs to be said even as you are standing there.*

Acts 1:8 *When the Holy Spirit has come upon you, you will receive power and will tell people about me everywhere—in Jerusalem, throughout Judea, in Samaria, and to the ends of the earth.*
The Lord gives us the Holy Spirit so that we have the power and courage to witness at all times and places.

How does the Holy Spirit help me?

1 Corinthians 2:12 *God has actually given us his Spirit (not the world's spirit) so we can know the wonderful things God has freely given us.*

We can call on the Spirit to help us understand the truth of God.

Romans 8:26-27 *The Holy Spirit helps us in our distress. For we don't even know what we should pray for, nor how we should pray. But the Holy Spirit prays for us with groanings that cannot be expressed in words. And the Father who knows all hearts knows what the Spirit is saying, for the Spirit pleads for us believers in harmony with God's own will.*

We can take great comfort and confidence in the fact that our prayers—as inadequate as they often are—are heard, understood, and acted upon through the loving intercession of the Holy Spirit.

1 Corinthians 6:19 *Don't you know that your body is the temple of the Holy Spirit, who lives in you and was given to you by God? You do not belong to yourself.*

Ephesians 5:18-20 *Don't be drunk with wine, because that will ruin your life. Instead, let the Holy Spirit fill and control you. Then you will sing psalms and hymns and spiritual songs among yourselves, making music to the Lord in your hearts. And you will always give thanks for everything to God the Father in the name of our Lord Jesus Christ.*

Because the Holy Spirit indwells us, he gives us the power and desire to resist other influences that would dishonor God or hurt us.

HOPE

What is my hope?

1 Peter 1:21 *Through Christ you have come to trust in God. And because God raised Christ from the dead and gave him great glory, your faith and hope can be placed confidently in God.*

The resurrection, the greatest event in history, is the foundation of our hope.

1 Peter 1:3-6 *All honor to the God and Father of our Lord Jesus Christ, for it is by his boundless mercy that God has given us the privilege of being born again. Now we live with a wonderful expectation because Jesus Christ rose again from the dead. For God has reserved a priceless inheritance for his children. It is kept in heaven for you, pure and undefiled, beyond the reach of change and decay. And God, in his mighty power, will protect you until you receive this salvation, because you are trusting him. It will be revealed on the last day for all to see. So be truly glad! There is wonderful joy ahead, even though it is necessary for you to endure many trials for a while.*

When people get motion sickness, they need to fix their eyes on the horizon in order to regain composure. Remaining fixed on a point in the distance helps us travel. Jesus' followers fix their eyes on an eternal horizon. This gives us hope in all the discomforts of daily life.

How can I have hope when times are tough?

Hebrews 10:23 *Without wavering, let us hold tightly to the hope we say we have, for God can be trusted to keep his promise.*

Our hope is rooted in God's integrity and faithfulness. When everything else falls apart we can cling to the fact that God keeps his word.

John 14:1 *Don't be troubled. You trust God, now trust in me.*

John 16:33 *I have told you all this so that you may have peace in me. Here on earth you will have many trials and sorrows. But take heart, because I have overcome the world.*

Our troubles do not surprise the Lord and should not surprise us. Trouble is rampant in this fallen world. Our focus should be on Jesus who has overcome this world and all its troubles.

Isaiah 26:3-4 *You will keep in perfect peace all who trust in you, whose thoughts are fixed on you! Trust in the LORD always, for the LORD GOD is the eternal Rock.*

Psalm 130:7 *O Israel, hope in the LORD; for with the LORD there is unfailing love and an overflowing supply of salvation.*

Psalm 146:5-10 *Happy are those who have the God of Israel as their helper, whose hope is in the LORD their God. He is the one who made heaven and earth,*

*the sea, and everything in them. He is the one who
keeps every promise forever, who gives justice to the
oppressed and food to the hungry. The LORD frees the
prisoners. The LORD opens the eyes of the blind. The
LORD lifts the burdens of those bent beneath their
loads. The LORD loves the righteous. The LORD protects
the foreigners among us. He cares for the orphans and
widows, but he frustrates the plans of the wicked. The
LORD will reign forever. O Jerusalem, your God is King
in every generation! Praise the LORD!*

Our hope is rooted in the wonderful acts of God
in creation and history. The Bible gives full
testimony to the fact that God is able to deliver us
from any and every circumstance. He will either
get us out of it or bring us through it—for his
glory and our joy.

Romans 15:13 *I pray that God, who gives you
hope, will keep you happy and full of peace as you
believe in him. May you overflow with hope through
the power of the Holy Spirit.*

Psalm 94:19 *When doubts filled my mind, your
comfort gave me renewed hope and cheer.*

Romans 5:1-5 *Since we have been made right in
God's sight by faith, we have peace with God because
of what Jesus Christ our Lord has done for us. Because
of our faith, Christ has brought us into this place of
highest privilege where we now stand, and we
confidently and joyfully look forward to sharing God's*

glory. We can rejoice, too, when we run into problems and trials, for we know that they are good for us—they help us learn to endure. And endurance develops strength of character in us, and character strengthens our confident expectation of salvation. And this expectation will not disappoint us. For we know how dearly God loves us, because he has given us the Holy Spirit to fill our hearts with his love. Expectation builds endurance. We can get through a great deal when we realize the wonderful gifts God has for us in this life and in the life to come.

How can I cultivate a stronger hope?

E p h e s i a n s 3 : 2 0 *Glory be to God! By his mighty power at work within us, he is able to accomplish infinitely more than we would ever dare to ask or hope.*
There is a sense in which we hope and expect too little from God. If we remind ourselves of the amazing things God has already done, we will know that we have reason to expect even more from the Sovereign Lord of the Universe.

HUMILITY

How does God respond to the humble?

P s a l m 2 5 : 9 *He leads the humble in what is right, teaching them his way.*

Humility means acknowledging our proper place before the Lord. When we humbly worship him, he will lead us and teach us the right way to live.

Psalm 149:4 *The LORD delights in his people; he crowns the humble with salvation.*

Matthew 23:12 *Those who exalt themselves will be humbled, and those who humble themselves will be exalted.*

Psalm 18:27 *You rescue those who are humble, but you humiliate the proud.*

Psalm 138:6 *Though the LORD is great, he cares for the humble, but he keeps his distance from the proud.*

Matthew 18:4 *Anyone who becomes as humble as this little child is the greatest in the Kingdom of Heaven.* The less we try to honor ourselves, the more God honors and blesses us. Pride builds barriers that keep God out of our lives. Humility opens the way for God to work because we are more willing to seek God's help and honor him for helping.

How does humility help me confront sin and evil?

James 4:6-10 *He gives us more and more strength to stand against such evil desires. As the Scriptures say, "God sets himself against the proud, but he shows favor to the humble." So humble yourselves before God. Resist the Devil, and he will flee from you. Draw close to God, and God will draw close to you. Wash your hands, you sinners; purify your hearts, you hypocrites. Let there be tears for the wrong things you have done. Let there be sorrow and deep grief. Let there be sadness instead of laughter, and gloom instead of joy. When you bow down before the Lord and admit your dependence on him, he will lift you up and give you honor.*

Pride gives the devil a key to our lives. Humility changes the lock and gives God the key. Humility comes from a godly sorrow for sin. We openly admit that we need God and seek his forgiveness. No proud person can do this.

How can humility help me in times of trouble?

1 Peter 5:6-7 *Humble yourselves under the mighty power of God, and in his good time he will honor you. Give all your worries and cares to God, for he cares about what happens to you.*

Daniel 10:12 *He said, "Don't be afraid, Daniel. Since the first day you began to pray for understanding and to humble yourself before your God, your request has been heard in heaven. I have come in answer to your prayer."*

The answer to all our problems is found in God's power and might, not our own abilities or resources. God hears and answers the prayers of the humble.

Isaiah 29:19 *The humble will be filled with fresh joy from the LORD. Those who are poor will rejoice in the Holy One of Israel.*

Isaiah 57:15 *The high and lofty one who inhabits eternity, the Holy One, says this: "I live in that high and holy place with those whose spirits are contrite and humble. I refresh the humble and give new courage to those with repentant hearts."*

When we turn to the Lord in humility, we find joy and refreshment. We no longer suffer under the burden of prideful expectations and loneliness. The Lord offers to carry our burdens for us, and we offer him our gratitude.

HUNGER FOR GOD

How does God respond to my hunger and longing?

Psalm 107:9 *He satisfies the thirsty and fills the hungry with good things.*

John 4:10-14 *Jesus replied, "If you only knew the gift God has for you and who I am, you would ask me, and I would give you living water." "But sir, you don't have a rope or a bucket," she said, "and this is a very deep well. Where would you get this living water? And besides, are you greater than our ancestor Jacob who gave us this well? How can you offer better water than he and his sons and his cattle enjoyed?" Jesus* replied, "People soon become thirsty again after drinking this water. But the water I give them takes away thirst altogether. It becomes a perpetual spring within them, giving them eternal life."

John 6:35 *Jesus replied, "I am the bread of life. No one who comes to me will ever be hungry again. Those who believe in me will never thirst."*

Too often we misunderstand our own desires. The things of this world will never satisfy the deepest longings of our hearts. The Lord alone can fulfill our longings because he built those longings into us.

How can I satisfy the deep longings of my life?

Matthew 6:31-33 *Don't worry about having enough food or drink or clothing. Why be like the pagans who are so deeply concerned about these things? Your heavenly Father already knows all your needs, and he will give you all you need from day to day if you live for him and make the Kingdom of God your primary concern.*

When we seek the Lord and order our lives according to his priorities, everything else falls into proper perspective. We can trust him to provide all we need.

Matthew 7:7 *Keep on asking, and you will be given what you ask for. Keep on looking, and you will find. Keep on knocking, and the door will be opened.*

Psalm 37:4-5 *Take delight in the LORD, and he will give you your heart's desires. Commit everything you do to the LORD. Trust him, and he will help you.* Faith does not mean inaction. The Lord invites us to earnestly pursue our godly desires. As we do, he promises to lead us into joy and satisfaction.

HURTS/HURTING

see Comfort, Suffering

INSECURITY

see also Confidence, Protection

How is God the solution to our insecurities?

Isaiah 43:1-4 *Now, O Israel, the LORD who created you says: "Do not be afraid, for I have ransomed you. I have called you by name; you are mine. When you go through deep waters and great trouble, I will be with you. When you go through rivers of difficulty, you will not drown! When you walk through the fire of oppression, you will not be burned up; the flames will not consume you. For I am the LORD, your God, the Holy One of Israel, your Savior. I gave Egypt, Ethiopia, and Seba as a ransom for your freedom. Others died that you might live. I traded their lives for yours because you are precious to me. You are honored, and I love you."*

We can feel insecurity in the face of life's dangers and threats and regarding our own worth and value. But all of these insecurities are addressed by God's promises. The Lord is our protector and our judge. We are loved beyond measure and protected in every circumstance.

How can I find security in who I am?

Zephaniah 3:17 *The LORD your God has arrived to live among you. He is a mighty savior. He will rejoice over you with great gladness. With his love, he will calm all your fears. He will exult over you by singing a happy song.*
The Lord delights in us! Like a father and mother rejoicing in the birth of a child, a bride and groom rejoicing over each other, or best friends celebrating after years of separation—so the Lord exults over us.

Matthew 5:13-16 *You are the salt of the earth. But what good is salt if it has lost its flavor? Can you make it useful again? It will be thrown out and trampled underfoot as worthless. You are the light of the world—like a city on a mountain, glowing in the night for all to see. Don't hide your light under a basket! Instead, put it on a stand and let it shine for all. In the same way, let your good deeds shine out for all to see, so that everyone will praise your heavenly Father.*
God has made us the salt and light of the earth. He has given us the privilege of influencing this world with the message of his love.

Romans 8:15-16 *You should not be like
cowering, fearful slaves. You should behave instead
like God's very own children, adopted into his
family—calling him "Father, dear Father." For his
Holy Spirit speaks to us deep in our hearts and tells us
that we are God's children.*
We are God's own children. When we let this
truth drown out our false feelings of
worthlessness, we find deep joy and lasting
security.

How does God protect me?

John 10:27-30 *My sheep recognize my voice; I
know them, and they follow me. I give them eternal
life, and they will never perish. No one will snatch
them away from me, for my Father has given them to
me, and he is more powerful than anyone else. So no
one can take them from me. The Father and I are
one.*
Our security comes from God's hold on us, not
our hold on God. Nothing can stand against his
power.

INTEGRITY

see also Character

How does God respond to my commitment
to integrity?

Psalm 18:20-25 *The LORD rewarded me for doing right; he compensated me because of my innocence. For I have kept the ways of the LORD; I have not turned from my God to follow evil. For all his laws are constantly before me; I have never abandoned his principles. I am blameless before God; I have kept myself from sin. The LORD rewarded me for doing right, because of the innocence of my hands in his sight. To the faithful you show yourself faithful; to those with integrity you show integrity.*

The psalmist claims a high level of personal integrity that makes some of us uncomfortable. It makes sense, however, when we realize that he isn't boasting in his accomplishment but thanking God for giving him the power and direction to live according to God's ways. This passage offers the same promise to us: God will empower our obedience.

1 Peter 2:12 *Be careful how you live among your unbelieving neighbors. Even if they accuse you of doing wrong, they will see your honorable behavior, and they will believe and give honor to God when he comes to judge the world.*

Our integrity may not bring immediate rewards, but we are certain that it will one day be recognized.

What are the benefits of integrity?

Proverbs 11:3, 5 *Good people are guided by their honesty; treacherous people are destroyed by their dishonesty. . . . The godly are directed by their honesty; the wicked fall beneath their load of sin.*

Integrity keeps us from the trap of dishonesty and the destruction that can result.

Psalm 15:1-5 *Who may worship in your sanctuary, LORD? Who may enter your presence on your holy hill? Those who lead blameless lives and do what is right, speaking the truth from sincere hearts. Those who refuse to slander others or harm their neighbors or speak evil of their friends. Those who despise persistent sinners, and honor the faithful followers of the LORD and keep their promises even when it hurts. Those who do not charge interest on the money they lend, and who refuse to accept bribes to testify against the innocent. Such people will stand firm forever.*

Our character affects our ability to worship and enjoy fellowship with God. Worship is more acceptable to God and more meaningful to us when we honor the Lord in our daily conduct.

How does the Lord enable us to seek integrity?

Proverbs 2:1-2, 5, 9 *My child, listen to me and treasure my instructions. Tune your ears to wisdom, and concentrate on understanding. . . . Then you will understand what it means to fear the LORD, and you will gain knowledge of God. . . . Then you will understand what is right, just, and fair, and you will know how to find the right course of action every time.*

141

God has given us the wisdom we need to lead lives that honor him. His word gives us the understanding, discernment, and motivation to choose the way of integrity.

John 14:15-21 *If you love me, obey my commandments. And I will ask the Father, and he will give you another Counselor, who will never leave you. He is the Holy Spirit, who leads into all truth. The world at large cannot receive him, because it isn't looking for him and doesn't recognize him. But you do, because he lives with you now and later will be in you. No, I will not abandon you as orphans—I will come to you. In just a little while the world will not see me again, but you will. For I will live again, and you will, too. When I am raised to life again, you will know that I am in my Father, and you are in me, and I am in you. Those who obey my commandments are the ones who love me. And because they love me, my Father will love them, and I will love them. And I will reveal myself to each one of them.*

Galatians 5:16-25 *I advise you to live according to your new life in the Holy Spirit. Then you won't be doing what your sinful nature craves. The old sinful nature loves to do evil, which is just opposite from what the Holy Spirit wants. And the Spirit gives us desires that are opposite from what the sinful nature desires. These two forces are constantly fighting each other, and your choices are*

*never free from this conflict. But when you are
directed by the Holy Spirit, you are no longer
subject to the law. When you follow the desires of
your sinful nature, your lives will produce these evil
results: sexual immorality, impure thoughts,
eagerness for lustful pleasure, idolatry, participation
in demonic activities, hostility, quarreling, jealousy,
outbursts of anger, selfish ambition, divisions, the
feeling that everyone is wrong except those in your
own little group, envy, drunkenness, wild parties,
and other kinds of sin. Let me tell you again, as I
have before, that anyone living that sort of life will
not inherit the Kingdom of God. But when the Holy
Spirit controls our lives, he will produce this kind of
fruit in us: love, joy, peace, patience, kindness,
goodness, faithfulness, gentleness, and self-control.
Here there is no conflict with the law. Those who
belong to Christ Jesus have nailed the passions and
desires of their sinful nature to his cross and
crucified them there. If we are living now by the
Holy Spirit, let us follow the Holy Spirit's leading
in every part of our lives.*

God has given us the Holy Spirit to conform us to
the image of Christ. He works in our hearts,
minds, and bodies to produce godly attitudes,
thoughts, and behavior.

JESUS CHRIST

Who is Jesus Christ?

2 Corinthians 1:19-20 *Jesus Christ, the Son of God, never wavers between yes and no. He is the one whom Timothy, Silas, and I preached to you, and he is the divine Yes—God's affirmation. For all of God's promises have been fulfilled in him. That is why we say "Amen" when we give glory to God through Christ.*

Jesus Christ is the promise of God! Through him all other promises are fulfilled.

What has Jesus promised to those who believe in him?

John 1:12 *To all who believed him and accepted him, he gave the right to become children of God.*

John 3:16-17 *God so loved the world that he gave his only Son, so that everyone who believes in him will not perish but have eternal life. God did not send his Son into the world to condemn it, but to save it.*

John 10:10 *The thief's purpose is to steal and kill and destroy. My purpose is to give life in all its fullness.*

Colossians 1:11-14 *We also pray that you will be strengthened with his glorious power so that you will have all the patience and endurance you need.*

144

May you be filled with joy, always thanking the Father, who has enabled you to share the inheritance that belongs to God's holy people, who live in the light. For he has rescued us from the one who rules in the kingdom of darkness, and he has brought us into the Kingdom of his dear Son. God has purchased our freedom with his blood and has forgiven all our sins. Jesus Christ is the Son of God who makes us sons and daughters of God through faith. He came to give us life—abundant and eternal.

Why can I have confidence in Jesus Christ?

Colossians 1:15-23 *Christ is the visible image of the invisible God. He existed before God made anything at all and is supreme over all creation. Christ is the one through whom God created everything in heaven and earth. He made the things we can see and the things we can't see—kings, kingdoms, rulers, and authorities. Everything has been created through him and for him. He existed before everything else began, and he holds all creation together. Christ is the head of the church, which is his body. He is the first of all who will rise from the dead, so he is first in everything. For God in all his fullness was pleased to live in Christ, and by him God reconciled everything to himself. He made peace with everything in heaven and on earth by means of his blood on the cross. This includes you who were once so far away from God. You were his enemies, separated from him by your evil thoughts and actions, yet now he has brought you back as his friends. He has done this through his death on the cross in his own human body. As a result, he has brought you into the very presence of God, and you are holy and blameless as you stand before him without a single fault. But you must continue to believe this truth and stand in it firmly. Don't drift away from the assurance you received when you heard the Good News. The Good News has been preached all over the world, and I, Paul, have been appointed by God to proclaim it.* These verses, some of the most powerful descriptions of Jesus Christ in the entire Bible, tell us that nothing is outside his control and that everything is possible through him. The more we know about Jesus Christ, the more confidence we have in him.

JOY

Where does joy come from?

Nehemiah 8:10 *Nehemiah continued, "Go and celebrate with a feast of choice foods and sweet drinks, and share gifts of food with people who have nothing prepared. This is a sacred day before our Lord. Don't be dejected and sad, for the joy of the LORD is your strength!"*

Zephaniah 3:17 *The LORD your God has arrived to live among you. He is a mighty savior. He will rejoice over you with great gladness. With his love, he will calm all your fears. He will exult over you by singing a happy song.*

Our joy springs from God's love, which is not dependent on circumstances nor on our performance. When we trust in his love for us, we are far less vulnerable to the depression and despair that could come from our problems and disappointments.

Revelation 21:4 *He will remove all of their sorrows, and there will be no more death or sorrow or crying or pain. For the old world and its evils are gone forever.*

Our joy is rooted in the certainty of heaven, where we will be fully and finally liberated from the trials and troubles of this life.

How can I be joyful in hard times?

Habakkuk 3:17-18 *Even though the fig trees have no blossoms, and there are no grapes on the vine; even though the olive crop fails, and the fields lie empty and barren; even though the flocks die in the fields, and the cattle barns are empty, yet I will rejoice in the LORD! I will be joyful in the God of my salvation.*

Philippians 4:4, 12 *Always be full of joy in the Lord. I say it again—rejoice! . . . I know how to live on almost nothing or with everything. I have learned the secret of living in every situation, whether it is with a full stomach or empty, with plenty or little.* Joy is a choice. We may not realize it, but we choose our moods and our attitudes. God's promises in Christ are the basis for choosing joy no matter what we face.

James 1:2 *Dear brothers and sisters, whenever trouble comes your way, let it be an opportunity for joy.*
Troubles remind us of two things: First, they remind us that this is a fallen world full of futility and frustration. Second, they remind us to turn to a God who will never disappoint us. God promises lasting joy for all those who believe in him. This kind of joy stays with us despite our problems.

2 Corinthians 4:14-18 *We know that the same God who raised our Lord Jesus will also raise us with Jesus and present us to himself along with you. All of these things are for your benefit. And as God's grace brings more and more people to Christ, there will be great thanksgiving, and God will receive more and more glory. That is why we never give up. Though our bodies are dying, our spirits are being renewed every day. For our present troubles are quite small and won't*

last very long. Yet they produce for us an immeasurably great glory that will last forever! So we don't look at the troubles we can see right now; rather, we look forward to what we have not yet seen. For the troubles we see will soon be over, but the joys to come will last forever. The promise of our future resurrection helps us look beyond the problems of daily life. It is not escapism or wishful thinking; it is a reality that fuels our joy by keeping things in perspective.

JUDGMENT

How will I be able to face the judgment of God?

Romans 5:9-10 *Since we have been made right in God's sight by the blood of Christ, he will certainly save us from God's judgment. For since we were restored to friendship with God by the death of his Son while we were still his enemies, we will certainly be delivered from eternal punishment by his life.* Our hope is based on the fact that Jesus Christ stood in our place for judgment. God no longer looks at us as enemies but as friends—even as his own children.

Romans 8:1-2 *Now there is no condemnation for those who belong to Christ Jesus. For the power of the life-giving Spirit has freed you through Christ Jesus from the power of sin that leads to death.*

Jesus Christ has relieved us from the threat of condemnation and death.

How does the future judgment affect my life now?

1 Corinthians 3:11-15 *No one can lay any other foundation than the one we already have—Jesus Christ. Now anyone who builds on that foundation may use gold, silver, jewels, wood, hay, or straw. But there is going to come a time of testing at the judgment day to see what kind of work each builder has done. Everyone's work will be put through the fire to see whether or not it keeps its value. If the work survives the fire, that builder will receive a reward. But if the work is burned up, the builder will suffer great loss. The builders themselves will be saved, but like someone escaping through a wall of flames.* The promise of salvation does not eliminate our responsibility. God has given us all that is necessary to lead meaningful, spiritually productive lives. We ignore his promises and provisions at great risk.

JUSTICE

What can I do when I suffer injustice?

Romans 12:17-19 *Never pay back evil for evil to anyone. Do things in such a way that everyone can see you are honorable. Do your part to live in peace* with everyone, as much as possible. Dear friends, never avenge yourselves. Leave that to God. For it is written, "I will take vengeance; I will repay those who deserve it," says the Lord.

Proverbs 20:22 Don't say, "I will get even for this wrong." Wait for the LORD to handle the matter.
God teaches us to respond differently to injustice than the world does. Vengeance and retribution are the way of the world. God teaches us to trust in him and allow him to settle the score.

How can I respond to persecution?

Matthew 5:11-12 God blesses you when you are mocked and persecuted and lied about because you are my followers. Be happy about it! Be very glad! For a great reward awaits you in heaven. And remember, the ancient prophets were persecuted, too.

2 Thessalonians 1:5-6 God will use this persecution to show his justice. For he will make you worthy of his Kingdom, for which you are suffering, and in his justice he will punish those who persecute you.
Persecution is part of what it means to be a follower of Jesus. God blesses those who bear dishonor and hardship for his sake.

LOVE

What are the benefits of loving God?

Deuteronomy 5:10 *I lavish my love on those who love me and obey my commands, even for a thousand generations.*

Deuteronomy 7:9 *Understand, therefore, that the LORD your God is indeed God. He is the faithful God who keeps his covenant for a thousand generations and constantly loves those who love him and obey his commands.*

This promise comforts us and inspires increasing gratitude and commitment to our gracious Lord. God's love and devotion literally reach across time to multiple generations.

What are the benefits of loving others?

Matthew 10:42 *If you give even a cup of cold water to one of the least of my followers, you will surely be rewarded.*

Hebrews 6:10 *God is not unfair. He will not forget how hard you have worked for him and how you have shown your love to him by caring for other Christians, as you still do.*

The Lord remembers us when we remember others. He rewards us for giving others kindness and practical help.

How will God help me love others more?

Galatians 6:8-10 *Those who live only to satisfy their own sinful desires will harvest the consequences of decay and death. But those who live to please the Spirit will harvest everlasting life from the Spirit. So don't get tired of doing what is good. Don't get discouraged and give up, for we will reap a harvest of blessing at the appropriate time. Whenever we have the opportunity, we should do good to everyone, especially to our Christian brothers and sisters.*

The Holy Spirit awakens our love for others. We can ask God to make us willing to love others—even those who are difficult—and God will hear our prayer.

LOVE OF GOD

How can I know God really loves me?

John 3:16 *God so loved the world that he gave his only Son, so that everyone who believes in him will not perish but have eternal life.*

1 John 3:1 *See how very much our heavenly Father loves us, for he allows us to be called his children, and we really are! But the people who belong to this world don't know God, so they don't understand that we are his children.*

1 John 4:7-12 *Dear friends, let us continue to love one another, for love comes from God. Anyone who loves is born of God and knows God. But anyone*

who does not love does not know God—for God is love. God showed how much he loved us by sending his only Son into the world so that we might have eternal life through him. This is real love. It is not that we loved God, but that he loved us and sent his Son as a sacrifice to take away our sins. Dear friends, since God loved us that much, we surely ought to love each other. No one has ever seen God. But if we love each other, God lives in us, and his love has been brought to full expression through us.

The gift of his son, Jesus Christ, is God's ultimate expression of his love for us. Though he gives many other blessings, he can give no greater gift.

Romans 5:5 *We know how dearly God loves us, because he has given us the Holy Spirit to fill our hearts with his love.*

The gift of the Holy Spirit is also an assurance of God's love. Though it may be difficult to prove objectively, the Spirit gives solid assurances in our hearts.

Romans 8:35-39 *Can anything ever separate us from Christ's love? Does it mean he no longer loves us if we have trouble or calamity, or are persecuted, or are hungry or cold or in danger or threatened with death? (Even the Scriptures say, "For your sake we are killed every day; we are being slaughtered like sheep.") No, despite all these things, overwhelming victory is ours through Christ, who loved us. And I am convinced that nothing can ever separate us from his love. Death can't, and life can't. The angels can't, and the demons can't. Our fears for today, our worries about tomorrow, and even the powers of hell can't keep God's love away. Whether we are high above the sky or in the deepest ocean, nothing in all creation will ever be able to separate us from the love of God that is revealed in Christ Jesus our Lord.* God promises that nothing can come between his love and us. Nothing!

What are the benefits of God's love for me?

Psalm 23:6 *Surely your goodness and unfailing love will pursue me all the days of my life, and I will live in the house of the LORD forever.*
We can be certain that God will continually shower us with his mercy and guard us in his love.

Psalm 31:7 *I am overcome with joy because of your unfailing love, for you have seen my troubles, and you care about the anguish of my soul.*
God understands our weaknesses and struggles without condemning us.

Psalm 103:8 *The LORD is merciful and gracious; he is slow to get angry and full of unfailing love.*

Hebrews 13:5 *Stay away from the love of money; be satisfied with what you have. For God has said, "I will never fail you. I will never forsake you."*

While we may struggle to keep loving, God never tires nor gives up on us. He is not subject to whims or moods or irritability or a bad temper. We can trust that his love is, indeed, unfailing. He will never turn his back on us.

How do I show my love for God?

John 15:10-11 *When you obey me, you remain in my love, just as I obey my Father and remain in his love. I have told you this so that you will be filled with my joy. Yes, your joy will overflow!*
Our obedience expresses our love for God. This should not be confused with earning God's love by good works. We obey God because we are already loved, not in order to be loved. And as we obey, we are promised joy.

MINISTRY

What is God calling me to do?

Matthew 9:37 *He said to his disciples, "The harvest is so great, but the workers are so few."*
People are ready to hear and receive the Good News of God's love. But with this promise comes the responsibility to work and to pray. The Lord expects us to enter fully into his work of reaching the world with the love of God.

Matthew 16:18-19 *Now I say to you that you are Peter, and upon this rock I will build my church, and all the powers of hell will not conquer it. And I will give you the keys of the Kingdom of Heaven. Whatever you lock on earth will be locked in heaven, and whatever you open on earth will be opened in heaven.*

As followers of Christ, we are part of the church, or the people of God. God has promised that we will overcome the kingdom of darkness and secure his victory. We must not be on the defensive, thinking we will one day lose. We should take the offensive and overcome evil with good.

How do I know God will help me minister for him?

Acts 1:8 *When the Holy Spirit has come upon you, you will receive power and will tell people about me everywhere—in Jerusalem, throughout Judea, in Samaria, and to the ends of the earth.*

When God calls, God equips. He has given us his promised Holy Spirit to help us fulfill the responsibility of telling the world about Jesus Christ.

1 Corinthians 12:4-7 *There are different kinds of spiritual gifts, but it is the same Holy Spirit who is the source of them all. There are different kinds of service in the church, but it is the same Lord*

157

we are serving. There are different ways God works in our lives, but it is the same God who does the work through all of us. A spiritual gift is given to each of us as a means of helping the entire church.

God has given every believer the gift of the Holy Spirit, and the Holy Spirit gives us his gifts as well. Great joy is ours as we share God's gifts with others.

Ephesians 4:11-13 *He is the one who gave these gifts to the church: the apostles, the prophets, the evangelists, and the pastors and teachers. Their responsibility is to equip God's people to do his work and build up the church, the body of Christ, until we come to such unity in our faith and knowledge of God's Son that we will be mature and full grown in the Lord, measuring up to the full stature of Christ.*

We often avoid the responsibilities of ministry because we think that ministry is reserved for professional ministers. But God has called all Christians to serve him, and he has promised that we will grow into maturity through faithful ministry.

What do I do if I am afraid or intimidated by ministry?

Matthew 28:18-20 *Jesus came and told his disciples, "I have been given complete authority in heaven and on earth. Therefore, go and make disciples of all the nations, baptizing them in the*

*name of the Father and the Son and the Holy Spirit.
Teach these new disciples to obey all the commands I
have given you. And be sure of this: I am with you
always, even to the end of the age."*
Jesus has been given all authority and has
promised to exercise it on our behalf. As we serve
him, we have the promises of his presence and
his power.

2 Timothy 1:7 *God has not given us a spirit of
fear and timidity, but of power, love, and
self-discipline.*
Fear comes when we believe the deceptions and
distortions of the evil one. Faith and
empowerment come from believing the promises
of God.

1 John 4:4 *You belong to God, my dear children.
You have already won your fight with these false
prophets, because the Spirit who lives in you is greater
than the spirit who lives in the world.*

Ephesians 6:10-11 *Be strong with the Lord's
mighty power. Put on all of God's armor so that you
will be able to stand firm against all strategies and
tricks of the Devil.*
Evil cannot intimidate us if we truly trust in the
Lord and make use of his provisions for us.

MISTAKES

see Failure

MONEY

see also Giving

Will God provide for my financial needs?

Matthew 6:31-33 *Don't worry about having enough food or drink or clothing. Why be like the pagans who are so deeply concerned about these things? Your heavenly Father already knows all your needs, and he will give you all you need from day to day if you live for him and make the Kingdom of God your primary concern.*

God knows our needs and promises to supply them fully. Worry denies or dismisses God's love and care. We can overcome anxiety by reminding ourselves of God's love and by pursuing God's will.

Philippians 4:11-13 *Not that I was ever in need, for I have learned how to get along happily whether I have much or little. I know how to live on almost nothing or with everything. I have learned the secret of living in every situation, whether it is with a full stomach or empty, with plenty or little. For I can do everything with the help of Christ who gives me the strength I need.*

Philippians 4:19 *This same God who takes care of me will supply all your needs from his glorious riches, which have been given to us in Christ Jesus.*

God promises to supply all of our needs. We must study God's word to discover what his definition of "need" is and what he says comprises a fulfilling life.

What are the benefits of using my money as God directs?

Proverbs 3:9-10 *Honor the LORD with your wealth and with the best part of everything your land produces. Then he will fill your barns with grain, and your vats will overflow with the finest wine.*

2 Corinthians 9:6-8 *Remember this—a farmer who plants only a few seeds will get a small crop. But the one who plants generously will get a generous crop. You must each make up your own mind as to how much you should give. Don't give reluctantly or in response to pressure. For God loves the person who gives cheerfully. And God will generously provide all you need. Then you will always have everything you need and plenty left over to share with others.*

We do not give in order to get, but we will often get when we give. When we are generous toward others, God is generous toward us.

Proverbs 11:24 *It is possible to give freely and become more wealthy, but those who are stingy will lose everything.*

God often blesses those who use money for his purposes. Those who hoard their money, using it only for themselves, never have enough.

Hebrews 13:5 Stay away from the love of money; be satisfied with what you have. For God has said, "I will never fail you. I will never forsake you."

1 Timothy 6:17-19 Tell those who are rich in this world not to be proud and not to trust in their money, which will soon be gone. But their trust should be in the living God, who richly gives us all we need for our enjoyment. Tell them to use their money to do good. They should be rich in good works and should give generously to those in need, always being ready to share with others whatever God has given them. By doing this they will be storing up their treasure as a good foundation for the future so that they may take hold of real life.

The secret to investing is knowing whom to trust and where to invest. The only lasting investment comes from trusting God and investing in others. Money can be a tool for blessing or a trap for deception. Use the resources God has given you to do good for others.

NEEDS

How can I be sure my needs will be met?

Psalm 23:1 The LORD is my shepherd; I have everything I need.

The starting point for our assurance is the promise of God's love. Even as sheep must depend fully on a good shepherd, we must depend fully on the Lord. He is eager to graciously lead us through life.

Romans 8:31-32 *What can we say about such wonderful things as these? If God is for us, who can ever be against us? Since God did not spare even his own Son but gave him up for us all, won't God, who gave us Christ, also give us everything else?*
If someone was offering you millions of dollars, you would not hesitate to ask them for just a few. God has met our greatest need by giving us his own Son to redeem us. Now, his great joy is in supplying all our other needs for the glory of his name.

Hebrews 4:16 *Let us come boldly to the throne of our gracious God. There we will receive his mercy, and we will find grace to help us when we need it.*
We should not hesitate to come to God because he welcomes our requests.

Philippians 4:19 *This same God who takes care of me will supply all your needs from his glorious riches, which have been given to us in Christ Jesus.*
God's resources far exceed my greatest needs.

Why does God promise to meet my needs?

2 Peter 1:3 *As we know Jesus better, his divine power gives us everything we need for living a godly life. He has called us to receive his own glory and goodness!*
The Lord supplies our needs so that we will grow in godliness. We learn to value God's priorities and learn not to be seduced by the world's value system. Our faith grows as we see the Lord's provision in action.

Matthew 6:33 *He will give you all you need from day to day if you live for him and make the Kingdom of God your primary concern.*

2 Corinthians 9:8 *God will generously provide all you need. Then you will always have everything you need and plenty left over to share with others.*

2 Kings 4:42-44 *One day a man from Baal-shalishah brought the man of God a sack of fresh grain and twenty loaves of barley bread made from the first grain of his harvest. Elisha said, "Give it to the group of prophets so they can eat." "What?" his servant exclaimed. "Feed one hundred people with only this?" But Elisha repeated, "Give it to the group of prophets so they can eat, for the LORD says there will be plenty for all. There will even be some left over!" And sure enough, there was plenty for all and some left over, just as the LORD had promised.*

God gives to us so that we will give to others. He is looking for vessels through whom he can express his love and care. Whether we have been richly blessed or have just enough to get by, the Lord promises there will always be enough to share.

OBEDIENCE

Why is obedience important to my spiritual life?

Deuteronomy 11:26-28 *Today I am giving you the choice between a blessing and a curse! You will be blessed if you obey the commands of the LORD your God that I am giving you today. You will receive a curse if you reject the commands of the LORD your God and turn from his way by worshiping foreign gods.*

The right thing to do is always the smart thing to do. God's commandments are not burdensome obligations but pathways to joyful, meaningful, satisfying lives. God's call for obedience is based on his own commitment to our well-being.

Exodus 19:5 *If you will obey me and keep my covenant, you will be my own special treasure from among all the nations of the earth; for all the earth belongs to me.*

Deuteronomy 7:9 *Understand, therefore, that the LORD your God is indeed God. He is the faithful God who keeps his covenant for a thousand generations and constantly loves those who love him and obey his commands.*

Jeremiah 7:23 *This is what I told them: "Obey me, and I will be your God, and you will be my people. Only do as I say, and all will be well!"*

John 14:15-16, 21-24 *"If you love me, obey my commandments. And I will ask the Father, and he will give you another Counselor, who will never leave you. . . . Those who obey my commandments are the ones who love me. And because they love me, my Father will love them, and I will love them. And I will reveal myself to each one of them." Judas (not Judas Iscariot, but the other disciple with that name) said to him, "Lord, why are you going to reveal yourself only to us and not to the world at large?" Jesus replied, "All those who love me will do what I say. My Father will love them, and we will come to them and live with them. Anyone who doesn't love me will not do what I say. And remember, my words are not my own. This message is from the Father who sent me."* Obedience is the visible expression of our love. Obedience to God is an intrinsic element of our covenant relationship with him. Sin is not about breaking the law but breaking God's heart.

What does God promise to those who obey?

Psalm 1:1-3 *Oh, the joys of those who do not follow the advice of the wicked, or stand around with sinners, or join in with scoffers. But they delight in doing everything the LORD wants; day and night they think about his law. They are like trees planted along the riverbank, bearing fruit each season without fail. Their leaves never wither, and in all they do, they prosper.*

Obedience paves the way for fruitfulness. When we obey, we have a clear conscience and uninterrupted fellowship with the Lord. We honor other people and stay out of conflict. We give our energies to things that last and do not waste time in unprofitable ways.

Psalm 84:11 *The LORD God is our light and protector. He gives us grace and glory. No good thing will the LORD withhold from those who do what is right.*

Even as a river flows freely through an unblocked channel, so God's grace and provision flow through us when we follow his ways.

How will the Lord help me to obey?

Philippians 2:12-13 *Dearest friends, you were always so careful to follow my instructions when I was with you. And now that I am away you must be even* more careful to put into action God's saving work in your lives, obeying God with deep reverence and fear. For God is working in you, giving you the desire to obey him and the power to do what pleases him. Where God requires us, God empowers us. God guides us in the ways that are best for us, and he gives us the power to live according to those ways.

John 14:15-17 *If you love me, obey my commandments. And I will ask the Father, and he will give you another Counselor, who will never leave you. He is the Holy Spirit, who leads into all truth. The world at large cannot receive him, because it isn't looking for him and doesn't recognize him. But you do, because he lives with you now and later will be in you.*
The power God gives us is his own Holy Spirit, our Counselor. He comes alongside us to advise us, inspire us, and actually live and work through us. Even as the breath we breathe empowers our physical bodies, so the Holy Spirit empowers our spiritual lives.

James 1:25 *If you keep looking steadily into God's perfect law—the law that sets you free—and if you do what it says and don't forget what you heard, then God will bless you for doing it.*
God's word sets us free from bondage to sin so that we can obey the Lord.

OPPORTUNITIES

How can I face challenging, sometimes intimidating, opportunities?

Philippians 4:13 *I can do everything with the help of Christ who gives me the strength I need.*
Our ability to face challenges is rooted in Christ, not in ourselves. With Christ's help, we can make the most of every opportunity.

Revelation 3:8 *I know all the things you do, and I have opened a door for you that no one can shut. You have little strength, yet you obeyed my word and did not deny me.*
We can trust that nothing will prevent us from fulfilling the opportunity God has for us.

How do I know if an opportunity is from the Lord?

Joshua 1:7-9 *Be strong and very courageous. Obey all the laws Moses gave you. Do not turn away from them, and you will be successful in everything you do. Study this Book of the Law continually. Meditate on it day and night so you may be sure to obey all that is written in it. Only then will you succeed. I command you—be strong and courageous! Do not be afraid or discouraged. For the LORD your God is with you wherever you go.*

169

Ephesians 5:15-20 Be careful how you live, not as fools but as those who are wise. Make the most of every opportunity for doing good in these evil days. Don't act thoughtlessly, but try to understand what the Lord wants you to do. Don't be drunk with wine, because that will ruin your life. Instead, let the Holy Spirit fill and control you. Then you will sing psalms and hymns and spiritual songs among yourselves, making music to the Lord in your hearts. And you will always give thanks for everything to God the Father in the name of our Lord Jesus Christ.

God's opportunities conform to his word. Anything that contradicts God's word is not an opportunity from God.

What does God promise to those who make the most of his opportunities?

Matthew 25:29 To those who use well what they are given, even more will be given, and they will have an abundance. But from those who are unfaithful, even what little they have will be taken away.

God honors faithfulness in little things with the privilege of responsibility for greater things.

PATIENCE

see also Hope

Where do I find the resources to be patient?

Galatians 5:22 *When the Holy Spirit controls our lives, he will produce this kind of fruit in us: love, joy, peace, patience, kindness, goodness, faithfulness.*
The Holy Spirit produces patience in our lives. As we relax and trust in him, we release our need to control life's circumstances.

Colossians 1:11 *We also pray that you will be strengthened with his glorious power so that you will have all the patience and endurance you need. May you be filled with joy.*
Prayer infuses patience into our lives. When we admit a need in prayer, the Lord begins to meet that need.

Psalm 37:34 *Don't be impatient for the LORD to act! Travel steadily along his path. He will honor you, giving you the land. You will see the wicked destroyed.*
Patience comes from simply trusting God day by day. Even when we don't think we can last very long, Christ gives us the strength to "travel steadily." Our commitments to faith and obedience will keep us on God's path for longer than we thought possible.

If God loves me, why do I have to wait patiently?

Daniel 10:12-13 *He said, "Don't be afraid, Daniel. Since the first day you began to pray for understanding and to humble yourself before your*

171

God, your request has been heard in heaven. I have come in answer to your prayer. But for twenty-one days the spirit prince of the kingdom of Persia blocked my way. Then Michael, one of the archangels, came to help me, and I left him there with the spirit prince of the kingdom of Persia."

Daniel prayed expectantly but had to wait because there was spiritual interference. We may not understand why God's response to our prayer seems delayed, but we can be assured that the Lord will overcome all opposition. Remember that from the time we begin to pray, God hears us.

Romans 5:3-5 *We can rejoice, too, when we run into problems and trials, for we know that they are good for us—they help us learn to endure. And endurance develops strength of character in us, and character strengthens our confident expectation of salvation. And this expectation will not disappoint us. For we know how dearly God loves us, because he has given us the Holy Spirit to fill our hearts with his love.* This world is God's waiting room. While we wait, we learn better how to live. We gain composure, strength, humility, and a deeper appreciation for God's care in our lives.

2 Peter 1:6-9 *Knowing God leads to self-control. Self-control leads to patient endurance, and patient endurance leads to godliness. Godliness leads to love for other Christians, and finally you will grow to have*

genuine love for everyone. The more you grow like this, the more you will become productive and useful in your knowledge of our Lord Jesus Christ. But those who fail to develop these virtues are blind or, at least, very shortsighted. They have already forgotten that God has cleansed them from their old life of sin. Patience is like a chisel, shaping godly character. It is like the Potter's hands, molding us into a vessel the Lord can best use. Teaching us patience is one of God's purposes in our lives.

What happens when I am patient?

Isaiah 40:31 *Those who wait on the LORD will find new strength. They will fly high on wings like eagles. They will run and not grow weary. They will walk and not faint.*
Waiting reveals our need for God's strength and gives God the opportunity to exercise his might on our behalf. As an athlete regains strength from sleep and time away from the contest, so we find strength by curtailing our own efforts and trusting the Lord to work. He will bring what we need when we need it.

Psalm 40:1 *I waited patiently for the LORD to help me, and he turned to me and heard my cry.*
Delays and difficulties are not signs that God is ignoring us. We can have hope and confidence in the knowledge that he hears our prayers in those hard times.

Habakkuk 2:3 *These things I plan won't happen right away. Slowly, steadily, surely, the time approaches when the vision will be fulfilled. If it seems slow, wait patiently, for it will surely take place. It will not be delayed.*

Our patience gives God time to work out his plan. God may seem to delay, but he is never late. His promises will come to pass in his perfect time.

Lamentations 3:25 *The LORD is wonderfully good to those who wait for him and seek him.*

Hebrews 10:36 *Patient endurance is what you need now, so you will continue to do God's will. Then you will receive all that he has promised.*

Those who give up, lose out. They are not being punished for giving up; they simply are absent when God works.

1 Peter 2:19-20 *God is pleased with you when, for the sake of your conscience, you patiently endure unfair treatment. Of course, you get no credit for being patient if you are beaten for doing wrong. But if you suffer for doing right and are patient beneath the blows, God is pleased with you.*

When we refuse to take things into our own hands, God takes them into his. God brings justice and vindication to those who wait on him.

PEACE

How can I find peace within?

Isaiah 9:6-7 *A child is born to us, a son is given to us. And the government will rest on his shoulders. These will be his royal titles: Wonderful Counselor, Mighty God, Everlasting Father, Prince of Peace. His ever expanding, peaceful government will never end. He will rule forever with fairness and justice from the throne of his ancestor David. The passionate commitment of the LORD Almighty will guarantee this!*

Lasting peace comes only from Jesus Christ, the Prince of Peace. He rules over all creation!

Psalm 3:5 *I lay down and slept. I woke up in safety, for the LORD was watching over me.*

Psalm 4:8 *I will lie down in peace and sleep, for you alone, O LORD, will keep me safe.*

Psalm 29:11 *The LORD gives his people strength. The LORD blesses them with peace.*

Psalm 32:7 *You are my hiding place; you protect me from trouble. You surround me with songs of victory.*

Our peace comes from knowing that we are under God's protection. As a watchman keeps guard over a city, so the Lord watches over us day and night.

Philippians 4:6-7 *Don't worry about anything; instead, pray about everything. Tell God what you need, and thank him for all he has done. If you do this, you will experience God's peace, which is far more wonderful than the human mind can understand. His peace will guard your hearts and minds as you live in Christ Jesus.*

Prayer is a gateway to peace. Our spirits lighten as we unburden our souls to the Lord. His peace is like a guard on patrol, protecting us from any assaults of anxiety or concern.

Isaiah 26:3 *You will keep in perfect peace all who trust in you, whose thoughts are fixed on you!*

We find peace when we remove our eyes from our problems and rivet our attention on our Lord.

Psalm 119:165 *Those who love your law have great peace and do not stumble.*

Peace comes from knowing and living according to the Scripture. God's wisdom and direction guide us into the ways of life and lead us out of conflict, compromise, and deception.

John 14:27 *I am leaving you with a gift—peace of mind and heart. And the peace I give isn't like the peace the world gives. So don't be troubled or afraid.*

Galatians 5:22 *When the Holy Spirit controls our lives, he will produce this kind of fruit in us: love, joy, peace, patience, kindness, goodness, faithfulness.*

The Holy Spirit brings peace into our lives.

How can I be at peace with others?

Psalm 34:14-15 *Turn away from evil and do good. Work hard at living in peace with others. The eyes of the LORD watch over those who do right; his ears are open to their cries for help.*
When we pursue peace with others, the Lord supports us in every way. He guards our steps and hears our prayers. We can pray confidently for him to change our own hearts and to touch the lives of those with whom we want to be reconciled.

Matthew 5:9 *God blesses those who work for peace, for they will be called the children of God.*
God blesses us as we seek to bring his peace to others.

Psalm 37:37 *Look at those who are honest and good, for a wonderful future lies before those who love peace.*
Bitterness and revenge can never bring lasting satisfaction. Anger and conflict will destroy our future. God promises a great future to those who make loving him and living at peace with others a way of life.

Proverbs 12:20 *Deceit fills hearts that are plotting evil; joy fills hearts that are planning peace!*
Seeking peace with others is one of the surest ways to release streams of joy and peace into our own hearts.

PERSISTENCE

see Endurance

PLANNING

How am I supposed to plan my life?

Proverbs 2:1-11 *My child, listen to me and treasure my instructions. Tune your ears to wisdom, and concentrate on understanding. Cry out for insight and understanding. Search for them as you would for lost money or hidden treasure. Then you will understand what it means to fear the LORD, and you will gain knowledge of God. For the LORD grants wisdom! From his mouth come knowledge and understanding. He grants a treasure of good sense to the godly. He is their shield, protecting those who walk with integrity. He guards the paths of justice and protects those who are faithful to him. Then you will understand what is right, just, and fair, and you will know how to find the right course of action every time. For wisdom will enter your heart, and knowledge will fill you with joy. Wise planning will watch over you. Understanding will keep you safe.* A plan is only as good as the information upon which it's based. Our human intellect is limited and inadequate. Apart from the Lord, our plans are liable to fail. The Lord promises wisdom to those who rely on his word and depend on his Spirit.

Proverbs 3:5-6 *Trust in the LORD with all your heart; do not depend on your own understanding. Seek his will in all you do, and he will direct your paths.*
As we seek God, he will guide us in making our plans.

What if my plans fall short of God's plans for me?

Proverbs 19:21 *You can make many plans, but the Lord's purpose will prevail.*
Our plans cannot mess up God's plans!

What gives me confidence in any plans?

Ephesians 1:9-10 *God's secret plan has now been revealed to us; it is a plan centered on Christ, designed long ago according to his good pleasure. And this is his plan: At the right time he will bring everything together under the authority of Christ—everything in heaven and on earth.*
God is in control of all things and always has been. Jesus Christ, who is now resurrected and ruling, will govern and guide us in the best possible ways.

Jeremiah 29:11 *"I know the plans I have for you," says the LORD. "They are plans for good and not for disaster, to give you a future and a hope."*
Do not doubt God's good intentions for us. The wonder of creation, the evidence of his constant care, and the priceless gift of Jesus Christ for our salvation give us confidence that he will establish all who trust in him.

POWER OF GOD

What is God's power like?

Psalm 20:4-7 *May he grant your heart's desire and fulfill all your plans. May we shout for joy when we hear of your victory, flying banners to honor our God. May the LORD answer all your prayers. Now I know that the LORD saves his anointed king. He will answer him from his holy heaven and rescue him by his great power. Some nations boast of their armies and weapons, but we boast in the LORD our God.*

God's power is greater than that of the greatest kings who ever ruled or the mightiest armies that ever marched. That power is ours as we trust him, obey him, and honor his name.

Psalm 44:4-7 *You are my King and my God. You command victories for your people. Only by your power can we push back our enemies; only in your name can we trample our foes. I do not trust my bow; I do not count on my sword to save me. It is you who gives us victory over our enemies; it is you who humbles those who hate us.*

God's power is greater than any of the skills or resources we have at our disposal. While we may use the means that God has provided to us, we know that victory comes from God alone.

How can God's power help me?

Psalm 60:12 *With God's help we will do mighty things, for he will trample down our foes.*
We should not look at the size of the problem but at the size of our God. When there are great things to be done, we have a great God who will do them through us.

Isaiah 40:29 *He gives power to those who are tired and worn out; he offers strength to the weak.*

2 Corinthians 12:9 *Each time he said, "My gracious favor is all you need. My power works best in your weakness." So now I am glad to boast about my weaknesses, so that the power of Christ may work through me.*
God's power does not depend on human strength and power. In fact, our resources can get in the way if we rely on them instead of on the Lord. God's power flows through our weaknesses like electric current through a wire. The wire is simply a conductor, with no power in itself. But without the wire, the current doesn't flow. God is looking for people who are wired for his service.

Acts 1:8 *When the Holy Spirit has come upon you, you will receive power and will tell people about me everywhere—in Jerusalem, throughout Judea, in Samaria, and to the ends of the earth.*

1 Peter 1:5 *God, in his mighty power, will protect you until you receive this salvation, because you are trusting him. It will be revealed on the last day for all to see.*

John 10:28-30 *I give them eternal life, and they will never perish. No one will snatch them away from me, for my Father has given them to me, and he is more powerful than anyone else. So no one can take them from me. The Father and I are one.*
God's power preserves and protects us until we reach our eternal home.

How can I experience God's power working through me?

Colossians 1:27-29 *It has pleased God to tell his people that the riches and glory of Christ are for you Gentiles, too. For this is the secret: Christ lives in you, and this is your assurance that you will share in his glory. So everywhere we go, we tell everyone about Christ. We warn them and teach them with all the wisdom God has given us, for we want to present them to God, perfect in their relationship to Christ. I work very hard at this, as I depend on Christ's mighty power that works within me.*

Philippians 2:13 *God is working in you, giving you the desire to obey him and the power to do what pleases him.*

1 John 4:4 *You belong to God, my dear children. You have already won your fight with these false prophets, because the Spirit who lives in you is greater than the spirit who lives in the world.*
God's power comes from his presence within us. We do not merely imitate Christ—trying through our own efforts to do right and seek God's will—we are indwelt by the living Lord.

Ephesians 6:10-12 *Be strong with the Lord's mighty power. Put on all of God's armor so that you will be able to stand firm against all strategies and tricks of the Devil. For we are not fighting against people made of flesh and blood, but against the evil rulers and authorities of the unseen world, against those mighty powers of darkness who rule this world, and against wicked spirits in the heavenly realms.*
Our spiritual growth is likely to stir spiritual opposition. Spiritual battles require spiritual power. God's armor provides power against the schemes of the world, the flesh, and the devil. Focus on the Lord's protection instead of the devil's threats and stand firm in the faith.

PRAYER

How can I know God hears my prayers?

Psalm 145:18 *The LORD is close to all who call on him, yes, to all who call on him sincerely.*

The Lord invites us to make prayer our first response rather than our last resort. He always listens to those who are honest with him.

2 Chronicles 7:14 *If my people who are called by my name will humble themselves and pray and seek my face and turn from their wicked ways, I will hear from heaven and will forgive their sins and heal their land.*

1 Peter 3:12 *The eyes of the Lord watch over those who do right, and his ears are open to their prayers. But the Lord turns his face against those who do evil.* Since prayer is a conversation with God, we must approach God with the same love and courtesy we bring to any relationship we value. We must be humble, not arrogant. We must admit our sin and seek God's forgiveness.

1 John 5:14-15 *We can be confident that he will listen to us whenever we ask him for anything in line with his will. And if we know he is listening when we make our requests, we can be sure that he will give us what we ask for.* While we may not know God's specific will for every situation, we do know that his will is to empower our obedience, to overcome evil with good, and to equip us to be his witnesses. We can pray confidently for his power and guidance, knowing that we are asking for the very things he most longs to give.

Why is prayer important?

Matthew 7:7-11 *Keep on asking, and you will be given what you ask for. Keep on looking, and you will find. Keep on knocking, and the door will be opened. For everyone who asks, receives. Everyone who seeks, finds. And the door is opened to everyone who knocks. You parents—if your children ask for a loaf of bread, do you give them a stone instead? Or if they ask for a fish, do you give them a snake? Of course not! If you sinful people know how to give good gifts to your children, how much more will your heavenly Father give good gifts to those who ask him.*

There's more to prayer than just getting an answer. God also does a work of grace in our own hearts through the act of prayer. As we persist in asking, seeking, and knocking, we gain greater a understanding of ourselves and of God.

How will God respond to my prayers?

Psalm 9:12 *He who avenges murder cares for the helpless. He does not ignore those who cry to him for help.*

Psalm 55:22 *Give your burdens to the LORD, and he will take care of you. He will not permit the godly to slip and fall.*

1 Peter 5:7 *Give all your worries and cares to God, for he cares about what happens to you.*

We experience freedom when we give a burden over to the Lord in prayer—even before the prayer is answered. The assurance of God's love and concern refreshes us and renews our hope.

Philippians 4:6-7 Don't worry about anything; instead, pray about everything. Tell God what you need, and thank him for all he has done. If you do this, you will experience God's peace, which is far more wonderful than the human mind can understand. His peace will guard your hearts and minds as you live in Christ Jesus.

There's no limit on prayer. Big requests, small requests, and all sizes in between are welcomed by God. If something bothers us, it should be brought to God.

PRESENCE OF GOD

Is it possible to experience God's presence today?

Hebrews 10:22-24 Let us go right into the presence of God, with true hearts fully trusting him. For our evil consciences have been sprinkled with Christ's blood to make us clean, and our bodies have been washed with pure water. Without wavering, let us hold tightly to the hope we say we have, for God can be trusted to keep his promise. Think of ways to encourage one another to outbursts of love and good deeds. *And let us not neglect our meeting together, as some people do, but encourage and warn each other, especially now that the day of his coming back again is drawing near.*

During Old Testament times, God's presence was expressed in limited ways. For example, the high priest could enter the Holy of Holies only once a year. In Jesus Christ, the veil between us and God is torn away, and we all enter freely into his presence. Let's not take for granted the privilege that is ours.

Ephesians 3:12 *Because of Christ and our faith in him, we can now come fearlessly into God's presence, assured of his glad welcome.*

Colossians 1:22 *Now he has brought you back as his friends. He has done this through his death on the cross in his own human body. As a result, he has brought you into the very presence of God, and you are holy and blameless as you stand before him without a single fault.*

When we have a free pass to an event, we do not hesitate to enter. We are given the privilege of admission based on the generosity of the giver. Our faith in Jesus Christ is God's free pass to his presence. When we put our trust in Jesus Christ, we can enter God's presence confidently.

Are there times or places when God leaves me?

Joshua 1:9 *I command you—be strong and courageous! Do not be afraid or discouraged. For the* LORD *your God is with you wherever you go.*

Matthew 28:20 *Teach these new disciples to obey all the commands I have given you. And be sure of this: I am with you always, even to the end of the age.* God does not come and go depending on his moods or circumstances. Knowing he is always with us can be a comfort in loneliness, a stimulus to obedience, a hedge against temptation, and a source of joy in his companionship.

Psalm 139:1-12 *O* LORD, *you have examined my heart and know everything about me. You know when I sit down or stand up. You know my every thought when far away. You chart the path ahead of me and tell me where to stop and rest. Every moment you know where I am. You know what I am going to say even before I say it,* LORD. *You both precede and follow me. You place your hand of blessing on my head. Such knowledge is too wonderful for me, too great for me to know! I can never escape from your spirit! I can never get away from your presence! If I go up to heaven, you are there; if I go down to the place of the dead, you are there. If I ride the wings of the morning, if I dwell by the farthest oceans, even there your hand will guide me, and your strength will support me. I could ask the darkness to hide me and the light around me to become night—but even in darkness I cannot hide from you. To you the night shines as bright as day. Darkness and light are both alike to you.*

Even when we feel distant from God he is there. The sooner we break with our denial, the sooner we will be able to deal with the things we are trying to hide and the intimacy that threatens us. The promise of God's presence holds the promise of our freedom.

Psalm 16:8, 11 *I know the LORD is always with me. I will not be shaken, for he is right beside me. . . . You will show me the way of life, granting me the joy of your presence and the pleasures of living with you forever.*

Psalm 23:6 *Surely your goodness and unfailing love will pursue me all the days of my life, and I will live in the house of the LORD forever.*

Isaiah 43:2 *When you go through deep waters and great trouble, I will be with you. When you go through rivers of difficulty, you will not drown! When you walk through the fire of oppression, you will not be burned up; the flames will not consume you.*

God's presence is like the sure hand of a guide who steadies us on a steep and slippery trail. We walk confidently because we know we are not walking alone.

Isaiah 46:4 *I will be your God throughout your lifetime—until your hair is white with age. I made you, and I will care for you. I will carry you along and save you.*
God's presence lasts a lifetime. He created us, sustains us, and will one day welcome us into his eternal presence.

Is God's presence affected by the presence of others?

Matthew 18:20 *Where two or three gather together because they are mine, I am there among them.*
The Lord gives a special promise to encourage and support us: We can experience God's presence in a special way through our fellowship with other believers.

How can we experience God's presence?

Psalm 145:18 *The LORD is close to all who call on him, yes, to all who call on him sincerely.*
The Lord invites us to call on him without hesitation. He will reveal himself to us.

James 4:8 *Draw close to God, and God will draw close to you. Wash your hands, you sinners; purify your hearts, you hypocrites.*
Sin drives a wedge between us and God. We must repent and be clean in order to be in full fellowship with him.

PROBLEMS

What do I do when problems overwhelm me?

Psalm 27:1 *The LORD is my light and my salvation—so why should I be afraid? The LORD protects me from danger—so why should I tremble?*
Problems can turn our eyes from the Lord. Use them, instead, as opportunities to turn our eyes to the Lord for his protection, his guiding light, and his saving power.

Psalm 145:14 *The LORD helps the fallen and lifts up those bent beneath their loads.*
God finds the fallen and never passes them by. When we feel we can't go another step, he shoulders our loads, easing our pain and burden.

Psalm 42:5-6 *Why am I discouraged? Why so sad? I will put my hope in God! I will praise him again—my Savior and my God! Now I am deeply discouraged, but I will remember your kindness—from Mount Hermon, the source of the Jordan, from the land of Mount Mizar.*
Remember God's mercy. He has been faithful in the past and will be faithful in the future. Memory ignites the fire of hope and drives away the darkness of despair.

How else does God care for me in times of trouble and danger?

Psalm 91:11 *He orders his angels to protect you wherever you go.*

Hebrews 1:14 *Angels are only servants. They are spirits sent from God to care for those who will receive salvation.*

In addition to all the other sources of help, God sends his mighty angels to watch over us. Though we rarely see them, we can trust God's word that they will care for us.

2 Corinthians 4:8-10 *We are pressed on every side by troubles, but we are not crushed and broken. We are perplexed, but we don't give up and quit. We are hunted down, but God never abandons us. We get knocked down, but we get up again and keep going. Through suffering, these bodies of ours constantly share in the death of Jesus so that the life of Jesus may also be seen in our bodies.*

God shows his care by his constant presence in our lives.

How can we help each other with our problems?

Galatians 6:2 *Share each other's troubles and problems, and in this way obey the law of Christ.* God works through others to show comfort and concern, to restore and refresh, to correct and challenge. While we each have burdens to bear, one of the great advantages of being a part of God's family is that we do not have to bear our burdens alone.

PROPHECY

What promises does God have for our future?

Matthew 24:30-31 *Then at last, the sign of the coming of the Son of Man will appear in the heavens, and there will be deep mourning among all the nations of the earth. And they will see the Son of Man arrive on the clouds of heaven with power and great glory. And he will send forth his angels with the sound of a mighty trumpet blast, and they will gather together his chosen ones from the farthest ends of the earth and heaven.*
One of the greatest promises in the Bible is that Jesus will come again. He will come in judgment—righting all wrong and vindicating his followers. We will be gathered together with him in heaven and enter into his glory.

1 Thessalonians 4:15-18 *I can tell you this directly from the Lord: We who are still living when the Lord returns will not rise to meet him ahead of those who are in their graves. For the Lord himself will come down from heaven with a commanding shout, with the call of the archangel, and with the trumpet call of God. First, all the Christians who have died will rise from their graves. Then, together with them, we who are still alive and remain on the earth will be caught up in the clouds to meet the Lord in the air and remain with him forever. So comfort and encourage each other with these words.*

When Jesus returns, he will secure the final victory for believers against Satan and all evil. We gain hope and strength as we remind ourselves that evil cannot and will not triumph.

How can I be confident that I will be ready for the future?

Jude 1:24 *All glory to God, who is able to keep you from stumbling, and who will bring you into his glorious presence innocent of sin and with great joy.*

2 Timothy 1:12 *That is why I am suffering here in prison. But I am not ashamed of it, for I know the one in whom I trust, and I am sure that he is able to guard what I have entrusted to him until the day of his return.*

God's hold on us—not our hold on him—is our ultimate basis for confidence. This does not diminish our call to trust and obey him, for we remember that we are saved by his grace alone.

PROTECTION

Where can I find protection and safety?

Psalm 121:2-8 *My help comes from the LORD, who made the heavens and the earth! He will not let you stumble and fall; the one who watches over you will not sleep. Indeed, he who watches over Israel never tires and never sleeps. The LORD himself watches over you! The LORD stands beside you as your protective shade. The sun will not hurt you by day, nor the moon at night. The LORD keeps you from all evil and preserves your life. The LORD keeps watch over you as you come and go, both now and forever.*
Our protection is directly related to the character, competence, and capability of our protector. The Lord is unsurpassed in all areas. The Maker of heaven and earth is our personal protector. He never sleeps and never turns his attention from us. We walk securely because he guards our every step.

1 Samuel 2:9 *He will protect his godly ones, but the wicked will perish in darkness. No one will succeed by strength alone.*

Job 5:19 *He will rescue you again and again so that no evil can touch you.*

Psalm 9:9 *The LORD is a shelter for the oppressed, a refuge in times of trouble.*
Though troubles and threats will find us in this fallen, rebellious world, they are not a surprise to the Lord. He never tires of saving us.

How does the Lord protect me?

Exodus 14:13-14 *Moses told the people, "Don't be afraid. Just stand where you are and watch the LORD rescue you. The Egyptians that you see today will never be seen again. The LORD himself will fight for you. You won't have to lift a finger in your defense!"*

Joshua 23:10 *Each one of you will put to flight a thousand of the enemy, for the LORD your God fights for you, just as he has promised.*

2 Chronicles 20:12, 15, 17, 20 *"O our God, won't you stop them? We are powerless against this mighty army that is about to attack us. We do not know what to do, but we are looking to you for help."* . . . *He said, "Listen, King Jehoshaphat! Listen, all you people of Judah and Jerusalem! This is what the LORD says: Do not be afraid! Don't be discouraged by this mighty army, for the battle is not yours, but God's. . . . You will not even need to fight. Take your positions; then stand still and watch the Lord's victory.*

He is with you, O people of Judah and Jerusalem. Do not be afraid or discouraged. Go out there tomorrow, for the LORD is with you!" . . . Early the next morning the army of Judah went out into the wilderness of Tekoa. On the way Jehoshaphat stopped and said, "Listen to me, all you people of Judah and Jerusalem! Believe in the LORD your God, and you will be able to stand firm. Believe in his prophets, and you will succeed."

When enemies come against us, they really come against the Lord. We are continually reminded that victory is assured when we let the Lord fight our battles. He can turn our enemies against each other so that they destroy themselves while we walk away unscathed.

Psalm 91:1-4 *Those who live in the shelter of the Most High will find rest in the shadow of the Almighty. This I declare of the LORD: He alone is my refuge, my place of safety; he is my God, and I am trusting him. For he will rescue you from every trap and protect you from the fatal plague. He will shield you with his wings. He will shelter you with his feathers. His faithful promises are your armor and protection.*

God guards us from the dangers that stalk us. God is a refuge, a shelter, and a place of safety from all threats. His promises shield us and inspire our faith and courage.

2 Thessalonians 3:3 *The Lord is faithful; he will make you strong and guard you from the evil one.* We gain spiritual strength from the Lord. He teaches us to protect ourselves through discernment, self-discipline, and the confident exercise of our authority in Christ.

Ephesians 6:10-12 *Be strong with the Lord's mighty power. Put on all of God's armor so that you will be able to stand firm against all strategies and tricks of the Devil. For we are not fighting against people made of flesh and blood, but against the evil rulers and authorities of the unseen world, against those mighty powers of darkness who rule this world, and against wicked spirits in the heavenly realms.* Spiritual battles require spiritual protection. God's armor shields us against the world, the flesh, and the devil. We must focus on the Lord's protection instead of evil's threats and stand firm in our faith.

PROVISION

see also Abundance, Giving, Money

Can I expect God to supply my needs?

Psalm 50:15 *Trust me in your times of trouble, and I will rescue you, and you will give me glory.* We can trust God to supply our needs.

Philippians 4:19 *This same God who takes care of me will supply all your needs from his glorious riches, which have been given to us in Christ Jesus.*

God's supplies are unlimited. He does not dole them out carefully but lavishes them on us according to his infinite grace.

How is Jesus Christ God's provision for me?

John 6:35 *Jesus replied, "I am the bread of life. No one who comes to me will ever be hungry again. Those who believe in me will never thirst."*

John 8:12 *Jesus said to the people, "I am the light of the world. If you follow me, you won't be stumbling through the darkness, because you will have the light that leads to life."*

John 10:9-10 *Yes, I am the gate. Those who come in through me will be saved. Wherever they go, they will find green pastures. The thief's purpose is to steal and kill and destroy. My purpose is to give life in all its fullness.*

John 10:14-15 *I am the good shepherd; I know my own sheep, and they know me, just as my Father knows me and I know the Father. And I lay down my life for the sheep.*

John 11:25-26 *Jesus told her, "I am the resurrection and the life. Those who believe in me, even though they die like everyone else, will live again. They are given eternal life for believing in me and will never perish. Do you believe this, Martha?"*

John 14:6 *Jesus told him, "I am the way, the truth, and the life. No one can come to the Father except through me."*

John 15:1, 5, 7-8 *I am the true vine, and my Father is the gardener. . . . Yes, I am the vine; you are the branches. Those who remain in me, and I in them, will produce much fruit. For apart from me you can do nothing. . . . If you stay joined to me and my words remain in you, you may ask any request you like, and it will be granted! My true disciples produce much fruit. This brings great glory to my Father.* Jesus is God's greatest provision for our greatest needs. He is our nourishment, our protection, our redeemer, our direction, our daily companion, and our eternal hope. He is our everything!

Romans 8:32 *Since God did not spare even his own Son but gave him up for us all, won't God, who gave us Christ, also give us everything else?* Since God gave us the ultimate gift in his Son, we can trust him for everything we need to live life for his glory.

PURPOSE/MISSION

Does God have a purpose for my life?

2 Timothy 1:9 *It is God who saved us and chose us to live a holy life. He did this not because we deserved it, but because that was his plan long before the world began—to show his love and kindness to us through Christ Jesus.*
Our purpose in life is rooted in God's eternal plan to redeem us and make us new creations in Christ for his glory and for his service.

John 15:16 *You didn't choose me. I chose you. I appointed you to go and produce fruit that will last, so that the Father will give you whatever you ask for, using my name.*
As we pursue our purpose in Christ, he promises that our lives will have lasting significance and eternal results.

1 Corinthians 15:58 *My dear brothers and sisters, be strong and steady, always enthusiastic about the Lord's work, for you know that nothing you do for the Lord is ever useless.*
As we pursue our God-given purpose, we do not get discouraged even when it seems that nothing is happening. God wastes nothing.

How can I discover my purpose and fulfill it?

Romans 12:1-2 *Dear brothers and sisters, I plead with you to give your bodies to God. Let them be a living and holy sacrifice—the kind he will accept. When you think of what he has done for you, is this too much to ask? Don't copy the behavior and customs of this world, but let God transform you into a new person by changing the way you think. Then you will know what God wants you to do, and you will know how good and pleasing and perfect his will really is.* Discovering God's purpose begins with a whole-hearted commitment to God. We give ourselves to the Lord because he has given everything to us. God promises to make his will known to us as we make ourselves available to him.

Philippians 1:20-22 *I live in eager expectation and hope that I will never do anything that causes me shame, but that I will always be bold for Christ, as I have been in the past, and that my life will always honor Christ, whether I live or I die. For to me, living is for Christ, and dying is even better. Yet if I live, that means fruitful service for Christ. I really don't know which is better.* When we commit ourselves to fulfilling God's purpose for our lives, the Lord promises that our lives will be fruitful. We will find meaning for ourselves and lead others to know the truth of Jesus Christ.

REGRETS

see Forgiveness

RELATIONSHIPS

see Belonging

RENEWAL

How can I find spiritual renewal and refreshment?

Psalm 32:3-5 *When I refused to confess my sin, I was weak and miserable, and I groaned all day long. Day and night your hand of discipline was heavy on me. My strength evaporated like water in the summer heat. Finally, I confessed all my sins to you and stopped trying to hide them. I said to myself, "I will confess my rebellion to the LORD." And you forgave me! All my guilt is gone.*

Psalm 51:10, 12 *Create in me a clean heart, O God. Renew a right spirit within me. . . . Restore to me again the joy of your salvation, and make me willing to obey you.*

Sometimes we are weary because we cling to sin and disobedience. Renewal comes through confession, repentance, and God's forgiving grace.

Ezekiel 36:26-27 *I will give you a new heart with new and right desires, and I will put a new spirit in you. I will take out your stony heart of sin and give you a new, obedient heart. And I will put my Spirit in you so you will obey my laws and do whatever I command.*

Renewal comes from a new heart and from the Holy Spirit. What was promised to Ezekiel was fulfilled in Christ.

How can I experience spiritual renewal on a more frequent, even continual, basis?

Psalm 23:3 *He renews my strength. He guides me along right paths, bringing honor to his name.*

God promises us spiritual refreshment if we dwell in his presence daily. Peace, confidence, and energy flow naturally from fellowship with the Lord.

Psalm 127:2 *It is useless for you to work so hard from early morning until late at night, anxiously working for food to eat; for God gives rest to his loved ones.*

God designed us to need and enjoy rest. Work is necessary, but not at the expense of rest. Faith means that we rest in God, trusting in his promise to provide for our needs.

Ephesians 4:21-24 *Since you have heard all about him and have learned the truth that is in Jesus, throw off your old evil nature and your former way of life, which is rotten through and through, full of lust and deception. Instead, there must be a spiritual renewal of your thoughts and attitudes. You must display a new nature because you are a new person, created in God's likeness—righteous, holy, and true.*

Colossians 3:10 *You have clothed yourselves with a brand-new nature that is continually being renewed as you learn more and more about Christ, who created this new nature within you.*

Through faith in Christ, we have the promise of becoming the kind of people that we really want to be. As we live according to the new nature that is ours in Christ, we experience spiritual refreshment and joy.

REPUTATION

Does God care about my reputation?

Colossians 3:23-24 *Work hard and cheerfully at whatever you do, as though you were working for the Lord rather than for people. Remember that the Lord will give you an inheritance as your reward, and the Master you are serving is Christ.*

What matters most is not what others think of us, but what God thinks of us (see Galatians 1:10). When we seek to please the Lord, he will give us favor with others.

What is the basis for my reputation?

1 Corinthians 1:30-31 *God alone made it possible for you to be in Christ Jesus. For our benefit God made Christ to be wisdom itself. He is the one who made us acceptable to God. He made us pure and holy, and he gave himself to purchase our freedom. As the Scriptures say, "The person who wishes to boast should boast only of what the Lord has done."*
Ultimately, we should be known not for what we have done but for what the Lord has done for us. We are "exhibit A" of God's greatness and goodness.

How can I maintain a godly reputation?

Proverbs 3:3-4 *Never let loyalty and kindness get away from you! Wear them like a necklace; write them deep within your heart. Then you will find favor with both God and people, and you will gain a good reputation.*
God promises to give a good name to those who show kindness, loyalty, and love to their neighbors.

Proverbs 22:1 *Choose a good reputation over great riches, for being held in high esteem is better than having silver or gold.*
God blesses the reputation of those who resist the temptation to trade their name and honor for wealth.

206

Romans 14:17-18 *The Kingdom of God is not a matter of what we eat or drink, but of living a life of goodness and peace and joy in the Holy Spirit. If you serve Christ with this attitude, you will please God. And other people will approve of you, too.*

Philippians 4:4-5 *Always be full of joy in the Lord. I say it again—rejoice! Let everyone see that you are considerate in all you do. Remember, the Lord is coming soon.*

Joy based on our confidence in Christ makes a powerful—and hopefully eternal—impression on others.

RESCUE

see also Challenges, Crisis

How will God rescue those who depend on him?

Psalm 91:9-16 *If you make the LORD your refuge, if you make the Most High your shelter, no evil will conquer you; no plague will come near your dwelling. For he orders his angels to protect you wherever you go. They will hold you with their hands to keep you from striking your foot on a stone. You will trample down lions and poisonous snakes; you will crush fierce lions and serpents under your feet! The LORD says, "I will rescue those who love me. I will protect those who trust in my name. When they call on me, I will answer; I will be with them in trouble. I will rescue them and honor them. I will satisfy them with a long life and give them my salvation."*

The Lord gives us absolute assurance: "I will rescue those who love me." This passage does not give us license to be reckless. But it gives us the promise that when people and circumstances turn against us, God is for us.

Psalm 6:4 *Return, O LORD, and rescue me. Save me because of your unfailing love.*

Psalm 50:15 *Trust me in your times of trouble, and I will rescue you, and you will give me glory.* God promises to rescue us not only for our welfare, but for his glory.

Psalm 72:12-14 *He will rescue the poor when they cry to him; he will help the oppressed, who have no one to defend them. He feels pity for the weak and the needy, and he will rescue them. He will save them from oppression and from violence, for their lives are precious to him.*

2 Corinthians 1:8-10 *I think you ought to know, dear brothers and sisters, about the trouble we went through in the province of Asia. We were crushed and completely overwhelmed, and we thought we would never live through it. In fact, we expected to die. But as a result, we learned not to rely on ourselves, but on God who can raise the dead. And he*

*did deliver us from mortal danger. And we are
confident that he will continue to deliver us.*
No situation is too difficult for the Lord. The
greater our need, the greater the depth of his love
and compassion is for us.

Why can't we depend on our own resources and rescue ourselves?

Psalm 33:16-22 *The best-equipped army cannot
save a king, nor is great strength enough to save a
warrior. Don't count on your warhorse to give you
victory—for all its strength, it cannot save you. But
the LORD watches over those who fear him, those who
rely on his unfailing love. He rescues them from death
and keeps them alive in times of famine. We depend
on the LORD alone to save us. Only he can help us,
protecting us like a shield. In him our hearts rejoice,
for we are trusting in his holy name. Let your
unfailing love surround us, LORD, for our hope is in
you alone.*
When trouble comes, our first reaction is usually
to try and solve the problem using our financial
assets, human connections, talents, and abilities.
Though these will all fail us in time, God never
will. God alone is our greatest defense. God alone
has the infinite resources we need.

Is there anything we can do to rescue ourselves?

2 Chronicles 7:14 *If my people who are called by my name will humble themselves and pray and seek my face and turn from their wicked ways, I will hear from heaven and will forgive their sins and heal their land.*

There are times when we bring problems on ourselves through our own disobedience. Our rescue depends on our faith and obedience. God calls us to humility and repentance to make way for his rescue.

How does God rescue us from the spiritual forces of evil and darkness?

Matthew 6:13 *Don't let us yield to temptation, but deliver us from the evil one.*

Prayer is a primary means by which God rescues us.

Ephesians 6:10-13 *Be strong with the Lord's mighty power. Put on all of God's armor so that you will be able to stand firm against all strategies and tricks of the Devil. For we are not fighting against people made of flesh and blood, but against the evil rulers and authorities of the unseen world, against those mighty powers of darkness who rule this world, and against wicked spirits in the heavenly realms. Use every piece of God's armor to resist the enemy in the time of evil, so that after the battle you will still be standing firm.*

Matthew 10:1 *Jesus called his twelve disciples to him and gave them authority to cast out evil spirits and to heal every kind of disease and illness.*
Though we are embroiled in a spiritual war with this world, we stand tall because we have full confidence in Christ's authority. We stand strong in the strength and protection of the Lord. This faith overcomes all fear.

REWARDS

see also Heaven

Are there rewards in this lifetime for following Jesus?

Psalm 84:11 *The LORD God is our light and protector. He gives us grace and glory. No good thing will the LORD withhold from those who do what is right.*

Hebrews 11:6 *It is impossible to please God without faith. Anyone who wants to come to him must believe that there is a God and that he rewards those who sincerely seek him.*
Knowing God brings rewards beyond anything this world offers. He promises to give every good thing to those who follow his way.

Matthew 6:4, 6, 17-18 *Give your gifts in secret, and your Father, who knows all secrets, will reward you. . . . When you pray, go away by yourself, shut the door behind you, and pray to your Father secretly. Then your Father, who knows all secrets, will reward you. . . . When you fast, comb your hair and wash your face. Then no one will suspect you are fasting, except your Father, who knows what you do in secret. And your Father, who knows all secrets, will reward you.*

Acts of devotion—such as giving, prayer, and fasting—bring the reward of knowing God more deeply and the satisfaction of acting honorably in his service.

Matthew 10:40-42 *Anyone who welcomes you is welcoming me, and anyone who welcomes me is welcoming the Father who sent me. If you welcome a prophet as one who speaks for God, you will receive the same reward a prophet gets. And if you welcome good and godly people because of their godliness, you will be given a reward like theirs. And if you give even a cup of cold water to one of the least of my followers, you will surely be rewarded.*

God blesses those who bless others. Acts of compassion and caring for others will surely be rewarded.

James 1:12 *God blesses the people who patiently endure testing. Afterward they will receive the crown of life that God has promised to those who love him.*

God gives the reward of eternal life to those who patiently and faithfully endure the difficulties, hardships, and tests they face in this life.

What are the rewards that await us in heaven?

1 Corinthians 2:9 *That is what the Scriptures mean when they say, "No eye has seen, no ear has heard, and no mind has imagined what God has prepared for those who love him."*
The best rewards we can imagine pale in comparison with what the Lord has in store for us.

Matthew 5:11-12 *God blesses you when you are mocked and persecuted and lied about because you are my followers. Be happy about it! Be very glad! For a great reward awaits you in heaven. And remember, the ancient prophets were persecuted, too.*
For those who suffer for their faith, heaven is more than compensation or vindication. It is fellowship with the Lord and all who have loved and honored him.

2 Timothy 4:7-8 *I have fought a good fight, I have finished the race, and I have remained faithful. And now the prize awaits me—the crown of righteousness that the Lord, the righteous Judge, will give me on that great day of his return. And the prize is not just for me but for all who eagerly look forward to his glorious return.*
Faithfulness to Christ brings an eternal reward of righteousness.

1 Peter 5:4 *When the head Shepherd comes, your reward will be a never-ending share in his glory and honor.*
Selfless service brings great rewards.

Hebrews 4:9 *There is a special rest still waiting for the people of God.*
The rest that is promised in heaven is not inactivity. It is the refreshment and satisfaction of savoring a completed, fulfilled work. Like an architect who enjoys living in a building that he or she designed, or a gardener who savors the fruits of hard labor, so will we enjoy the rest and refreshment of the Lord's work in our life.

SALVATION

see also Grace

What does it mean to be saved?

Romans 4:4-8 *When people work, their wages are not a gift. Workers earn what they receive. But people are declared righteous because of their faith, not because of their work. King David spoke of this, describing the happiness of an undeserving sinner who is declared to be righteous: "Oh, what joy for those whose disobedience is forgiven, whose sins are put out of sight. Yes, what joy for those whose sin is no longer counted against them by the Lord."*

Romans 3:24 *Now God in his gracious kindness declares us not guilty. He has done this through Christ Jesus, who has freed us by taking away our sins.* God promises to forgive our sins and restore us to full fellowship with him if we put our trust in Jesus Christ. Being saved means no longer having our sins count against us; it means being forgiven by the grace of God and being given eternal life.

Psalm 103:11-12 *His unfailing love toward those who fear him is as great as the height of the heavens above the earth. He has removed our rebellious acts as far away from us as the east is from the west.* Being saved means our sins have been completely removed.

How can I be saved from eternal death and separation from God?

John 3:16-18 *God so loved the world that he gave his only Son, so that everyone who believes in him will not perish but have eternal life. God did not send his Son into the world to condemn it, but to save it. There is no judgment awaiting those who trust him. But those who do not trust him have already been judged for not believing in the only Son of God.*

Romans 3:20-22 *No one can ever be made right in God's sight by doing what his law commands. For the more we know God's law, the clearer it becomes that we aren't obeying it. But now God has shown us a different way of being right in his sight—not by obeying the law but by the way promised in the Scriptures long ago. We are made right in God's sight when we trust in Jesus Christ to take away our sins. And we all can be saved in this same way, no matter who we are or what we have done.*

God sent Jesus Christ to take our place and receive the punishment for sin that we deserved. When we trust in him, we receive the gifts of eternal life and fellowship with God.

Romans 10:9-10 *If you confess with your mouth that Jesus is Lord and believe in your heart that God raised him from the dead, you will be saved. For it is by believing in your heart that you are made right with God, and it is by confessing with your mouth that you are saved.*

Ephesians 2:8 *God saved you by his special favor when you believed. And you can't take credit for this; it is a gift from God.*

We are saved by faith, putting our confidence and trust in what God has done for us in Christ.

Does the Lord want to save me?

Isaiah 59:1 *Listen! The LORD is not too weak to save you, and he is not becoming deaf. He can hear you when you call.*

2 Peter 3:9 *The Lord isn't really being slow about his promise to return, as some people think. No, he is being patient for your sake. He does not want anyone to perish, so he is giving more time for everyone to repent.*

Yes! God has both the power and the desire to save all who call upon him.

How does salvation affect my daily life?

2 Corinthians 5:17 *What this means is that those who become Christians become new persons. They are not the same anymore, for the old life is gone. A new life has begun!*
Salvation not only gives us hope for eternity, but also hope for today. We have been given a new life and new power for living.

Romans 6:6-8 *Our old sinful selves were crucified with Christ so that sin might lose its power in our lives. We are no longer slaves to sin. For when we died with Christ we were set free from the power of sin. And since we died with Christ, we know we will also share his new life.*
Being saved means being freed from the power of sin and being free to live a new life.

Romans 5:1-2 *Since we have been made right in God's sight by faith, we have peace with God because of what Jesus Christ our Lord has done for us. Because of our faith, Christ has brought us into this place of highest privilege where we now stand, and we confidently and joyfully look forward to sharing God's glory.*
Salvation brings peace with God.

Ephesians 2:8-10 *God saved you by his special favor when you believed. And you can't take credit for this; it is a gift from God. Salvation is not a reward for the good things we have done, so none of us can boast about it. For we are God's masterpiece. He has created us anew in Christ Jesus, so that we can do the good things he planned for us long ago.*

God created us for a purpose. Salvation enables us to fulfill that purpose through the power of God at work within us.

SANCTIFICATION

see Holy/Holiness

SELF-CONTROL

see also Habits, Power of God, Temptation

Is it possible to exercise self-control?

2 Peter 1:6 *Knowing God leads to self-control. Self-control leads to patient endurance, and patient endurance leads to godliness.*

Self-control is possible only through God. According to the Bible, sin reigns in our lives, controlling us completely, until Jesus Christ breaks its power.

2 Corinthians 3:17 *The Lord is the Spirit, and wherever the Spirit of the Lord is, he gives freedom.*

Galatians 5:22-23 *When the Holy Spirit controls our lives, he will produce this kind of fruit in us: love, joy, peace, patience, kindness, goodness, faithfulness, gentleness, and self-control. Here there is no conflict with the law.*

Self-control is promised through the power of the Holy Spirit. He works within us to bring freedom from the drives and desires that distract us from living for God.

What are some steps to exercising self-control?

Psalm 119:9 *How can a young person stay pure? By obeying your word and following its rules.*

Studying God's word shows us how to exercise self-control. God's word guides and empowers our obedience. God's promises awaken hope. God's commands give wisdom and direction.

1 Timothy 4:7-10 *Do not waste time arguing over godless ideas and old wives' tales. Spend your time and energy in training yourself for spiritual fitness. Physical exercise has some value, but spiritual exercise is much more important, for it promises a reward in both this life and the next. This is true, and everyone should accept it. We work hard and suffer much in order that people will believe the truth, for our hope is in the living God, who is the Savior of all people, and particularly of those who believe.*

Self-control begins with God's work within us, but it requires our effort as well. A talented musician or athlete must develop their talent, strength, and coordination through intentional effort. God promises to reward such effort far beyond any investment we make.

1 Corinthians 10:13 *Remember that the temptations that come into your life are no different from what others experience. And God is faithful. He will keep the temptation from becoming so strong that you can't stand up against it. When you are tempted, he will show you a way out so that you will not give in to it.* We are all subject to the same trials and temptations. Instead of thinking that resistance is futile, we should call on the Lord to lead us out of temptation. He promises to give us what we need in order to resist.

SICKNESS

see Healing, Suffering

STRENGTH

How can I experience God's strength in my life?

Nehemiah 8:10 *Nehemiah continued, "Go and celebrate with a feast of choice foods and sweet drinks, and share gifts of food with people who have nothing*

220

prepared. This is a sacred day before our Lord. Don't be dejected and sad, for the joy of the LORD is your strength!" Strength starts in the heart long before it is exerted in other aspects of life. The joy of the Lord gives us strength to obey, to endure, and to triumph in all circumstances.

Isaiah 40:29, 31 *He gives power to those who are tired and worn out; he offers strength to the weak. . . . Those who wait on the LORD will find new strength. They will fly high on wings like eagles. They will run and not grow weary. They will walk and not faint.* Life wears us out, but waiting on the Lord renews our strength. Our limitations remind us to rely more fully on the Lord.

Psalm 138:3 *When I pray, you answer me; you encourage me by giving me the strength I need.* God's strength comes through prayer.

What can I do in God's strength?

Philippians 4:13 *I can do everything with the help of Christ who gives me the strength I need.* There are no limits to what God can do in and through us.

Psalm 18:1-2, 29-30 *I love you, LORD; you are my strength. The LORD is my rock, my fortress, and my savior; my God is my rock, in whom I find protection. He is my shield, the strength of my salvation, and my stronghold. . . . In your strength I can crush an army; with my God I can scale any wall. As for God, his way is perfect. All the LORD's promises prove true. He is a shield for all who look to him for protection.*

Ephesians 3:20 *Now glory be to God! By his mighty power at work within us, he is able to accomplish infinitely more than we would ever dare to ask or hope.*

God's strength in us is a result of his love for us. In his strength we have the power to do things that we could never do on our own. We can withstand the toughest attacks and can take the offensive to overcome our problems.

Psalm 46:1-2 *God is our refuge and strength, always ready to help in times of trouble. So we will not fear, even if earthquakes come and the mountains crumble into the sea.*

By God's strength we can live without fear, because God's strength drives out fear.

STRESS

see also Peace

Should I be surprised by the stress of life?

John 16:33 *I have told you all this so that you may have peace in me. Here on earth you will have many trials and sorrows. But take heart, because I have overcome the world.*

Jesus warned us to expect stress. This world is filled with trials and sorrows that generate stress in our lives. Christ gives us lasting peace because his power and grace are able to overcome all sources of stress in our lives.

What can I do to find relief from stress and anxiety?

Isaiah 41:10 *Don't be afraid, for I am with you. Do not be dismayed, for I am your God. I will strengthen you. I will help you. I will uphold you with my victorious right hand.*
We can turn from fear and anxiety to faith and peace. God promises to supply the power to get us through the hard times.

Matthew 11:28-29 *Jesus said, "Come to me, all of you who are weary and carry heavy burdens, and I will give you rest. Take my yoke upon you. Let me teach you, because I am humble and gentle, and you will find rest for your souls."*
Resting in Christ breaks the hold of stress. When we are yoked together in service to him, we are free from the unrealistic and destructive expectations that can overwhelm us. Jesus' humility and gentleness overcome every conflict and stress in this life.

What do we learn from stress?

2 Corinthians 1:8-9 *I think you ought to know, dear brothers and sisters, about the trouble we went through in the province of Asia. We were crushed and completely overwhelmed, and we thought we would never live through it. In fact, we expected to die. But as a result, we learned not to rely on ourselves, but on God who can raise the dead.*
Stress exposes our human limitations so that we can better realize God's limitless power and love.

Galatians 6:9 *Don't get tired of doing what is good. Don't get discouraged and give up, for we will reap a harvest of blessing at the appropriate time.*
We keep going because God has promised a rich harvest in his perfect time.

Romans 5:3-4 *We can rejoice, too, when we run into problems and trials, for we know that they are good for us—they help us learn to endure. And endurance develops strength of character in us, and character strengthens our confident expectation of salvation.*

James 1:2-4 *Dear brothers and sisters, whenever trouble comes your way, let it be an opportunity for joy. For when your faith is tested, your endurance has a chance to grow. So let it grow, for when your endurance is fully developed, you will be strong in character and ready for anything.*

While stress exposes our true character, it also
helps develop our true character. Even when we
fall short of the mark, God has promised to work
within us, shaping us into the image of Christ.

SUCCESS

Does God promise us success in this life?

1 Samuel 16:7 *The LORD said to Samuel, "Don't
judge by his appearance or height, for I have rejected
him. The LORD doesn't make decisions the way you
do! People judge by outward appearance, but the
LORD looks at a person's thoughts and intentions."*
God's standards differ greatly from our own. Success
is measured by faithfulness and fruitfulness not by
results and quantities. We measure success in terms
of appearances and externals, but the Lord looks on
the heart. God measures success by weighing our
devotion and commitment to him.

1 John 2:15-17 *Stop loving this evil world and
all that it offers you, for when you love the world, you
show that you do not have the love of the Father in
you. For the world offers only the lust for physical
pleasure, the lust for everything we see, and pride in
our possessions. These are not from the Father. They
are from this evil world. And this world is fading
away, along with everything it craves. But if you do
the will of God, you will live forever.*

Success in this world can mean failure in God's eyes. While we live in this world, we are not to be controlled by this world's system of values. God promises that if we do his will, we will have true success.

2 Corinthians 3:4-5 *We are confident of all this because of our great trust in God through Christ. It is not that we think we can do anything of lasting value by ourselves. Our only power and success come from God.*
Jesus' followers know that real success comes only from the Lord.

How can we succeed in God's eyes?

Joshua 1:8-9 *Study this Book of the Law continually. Meditate on it day and night so you may be sure to obey all that is written in it. Only then will you succeed. I command you—be strong and courageous! Do not be afraid or discouraged. For the LORD your God is with you wherever you go.*
God's word is our guide to success. It teaches us the truth and equips us with the skills and understanding to live life to the fullest.

Deuteronomy 30:6-9 *The LORD your God will cleanse your heart and the hearts of all your descendants so that you will love him with all your heart and soul, and so you may live! The LORD your God will inflict all these curses on your enemies and persecutors. Then you will again obey the LORD and keep all the commands I*

226

am giving you today. The LORD your God will make you successful in everything you do. He will give you many children and numerous livestock, and your fields will produce abundant harvests, for the LORD will delight in being good to you as he was to your ancestors.

Pleasing God is the key to success. The Lord blesses those who obey, because they live according to his intentions for them. God works in our hearts to make us spiritually successful.

How can I pursue success God's way?

Proverbs 16:3 *Commit your work to the LORD, and then your plans will succeed.*
The first step toward success is committing all that we do to God.

Proverbs 15:22 *Plans go wrong for lack of advice; many counselors bring success.*
Another step toward success is trusting God to guide us through the wise counsel of godly people.

Proverbs 21:31 *The horses are prepared for battle, but the victory belongs to the LORD.*

Psalm 44:3-4 *They did not conquer the land with their swords; it was not their own strength that gave them victory. It was by your mighty power that they succeeded; it was because you favored them and smiled on them. You are my King and my God. You command victories for your people.*

God is the one who gives success. We may be as prepared and diligent as humanly possible, but we should never trust in our preparation or our resources. We trust the promises and power of God alone.

Psalm 112:1-4 *Praise the LORD! Happy are those who fear the LORD. Yes, happy are those who delight in doing what he commands. Their children will be successful everywhere; an entire generation of godly people will be blessed. They themselves will be wealthy, and their good deeds will never be forgotten. When darkness overtakes the godly, light will come bursting in. They are generous, compassionate, and righteous.*
Faithfulness bears fruit for generations to come. God's grace is far more reliable than any earthly treasures or titles. He promises to leave a spiritual legacy of success to our families—there is no better inheritance.

SUFFERING

Does suffering mean God doesn't care about me?

Psalm 22:24 *He has not ignored the suffering of the needy. He has not turned and walked away. He has listened to their cries for help.*

Suffering is not a sign of God's absence; it is a fact of life in this fallen world. God is with us in the midst of life's struggles. He may not remove them from us, but he does promise to help us get through them.

Psalm 56:8-9 *You keep track of all my sorrows. You have collected all my tears in your bottle. You have recorded each one in your book. On the very day I call to you for help, my enemies will retreat. This I know: God is on my side.*

God's care is such that not even a single tear goes unnoticed. He knows our every pain and will one day lead us to victory.

1 Peter 4:13-17 *Be very glad—because these trials will make you partners with Christ in his suffering, and afterward you will have the wonderful joy of sharing his glory when it is displayed to all the world. Be happy if you are insulted for being a Christian, for then the glorious Spirit of God will come upon you. If you suffer, however, it must not be for murder, stealing, making trouble, or prying into other people's affairs. But it is no shame to suffer for being a Christian. Praise God for the privilege of being called by his wonderful name! For the time has come for judgment, and it must begin first among God's own children. And if even we Christians must be judged, what terrible fate awaits those who have never believed God's Good News?*

John 16:33 *I have told you all this so that you may have peace in me. Here on earth you will have many trials and sorrows. But take heart, because I have overcome the world.*

We will suffer for what we believe. Whether we are mocked, teased, ignored, or physically harmed, the Lord notices and will reward us. If we are not ashamed of him, he will not be ashamed of us.

What are God's promises in the midst of suffering?

Isaiah 43:1-2 *Now, O Israel, the LORD who created you says: "Do not be afraid, for I have ransomed you. I have called you by name; you are mine. When you go through deep waters and great trouble, I will be with you. When you go through rivers of difficulty, you will not drown! When you walk through the fire of oppression, you will not be burned up; the flames will not consume you."*

We belong to the Lord. He knows us by name and will not allow anything to cause us lasting harm. We may go through deep waters of trouble and intense fires of trial and testing, but we will not go through them alone.

Romans 8:38-39 *I am convinced that nothing can ever separate us from his love. Death can't, and life can't. The angels can't, and the demons can't. Our fears for today, our worries about tomorrow, and even the powers of hell can't keep God's love away. Whether we are high above the sky or in the deepest ocean, nothing in all creation will ever be able to separate us from the love of God that is revealed in Christ Jesus our Lord.*

The greatest comfort in life is knowing that God will never leave us. Nothing can drive us from his presence. No matter what we are going through, he is there to comfort, sustain, encourage, and direct us.

Psalm 147:3 *He heals the brokenhearted, binding up their wounds.*

Psalm 30:5 *His anger lasts for a moment, but his favor lasts a lifetime! Weeping may go on all night, but joy comes with the morning.*

Psalm 126:5-6 *Those who plant in tears will harvest with shouts of joy. They weep as they go to plant their seed, but they sing as they return with the harvest.*

Nothing lasts forever. Sometimes the only thing that keeps us going is the reminder that this time of suffering will also pass. We trust that one day we will look back and it will be a memory. Hopefully, it will also be a testimony to God's faithfulness and a reason for rejoicing.

2 Corinthians 1:3-5 *All praise to the God and Father of our Lord Jesus Christ. He is the source of every mercy and the God who comforts us. He comforts*

231

us in all our troubles so that we can comfort others. When others are troubled, we will be able to give them the same comfort God has given us. You can be sure that the more we suffer for Christ, the more God will shower us with his comfort through Christ.

Our suffering makes us more sensitive to God's presence in our lives and to the suffering of others.

R o m a n s 5 : 3 - 4 *We can rejoice, too, when we run into problems and trials, for we know that they are good for us—they help us learn to endure. And endurance develops strength of character in us, and character strengthens our confident expectation of salvation.*

J a m e s 1 : 3 - 4 *When your faith is tested, your endurance has a chance to grow. So let it grow, for when your endurance is fully developed, you will be strong in character and ready for anything.*

Suffering teaches us lessons that we can learn no other way. As we look to the Lord, he promises to bring good fruit from hard times.

TEMPTATION

see also Addiction, Evil, Holy/Holiness, Self-Control

Do I have the power to resist overwhelming temptation?

M a t t h e w 4 : 5 - 7 *The Devil took him to Jerusalem, to the highest point of the Temple, and* said, "If you are the Son of God, jump off! For the Scriptures say, 'He orders his angels to protect you. And they will hold you with their hands to keep you from striking your foot on a stone.'" Jesus responded, "The Scriptures also say, 'Do not test the Lord your God.'"

James 4:7 *Humble yourselves before God. Resist the Devil, and he will flee from you.*
The devil can tempt us, but we can resist him just as Jesus did—by responding to the temptation with the truth of God's word.

1 John 4:4 *You belong to God, my dear children. You have already won your fight with these false prophets, because the Spirit who lives in you is greater than the spirit who lives in the world.*

1 John 5:4-5 *Every child of God defeats this evil world by trusting Christ to give the victory. And the ones who win this battle against the world are the ones who believe that Jesus is the Son of God.*
We can break free from temptation when we change our focus and our minds. Instead of thinking about our weakness, we can fill our minds with the promise of God's strength. In Christ we have power. We must never forget that the Holy Spirit is great enough to overcome any threat against us.

Jude 1:24-25 *Now, all glory to God, who is able to keep you from stumbling, and who will bring you into his glorious presence innocent of sin and with great joy. All glory to him, who alone is God our Savior, through Jesus Christ our Lord. Yes, glory, majesty, power, and authority belong to him, in the beginning, now, and forevermore. Amen.*

Our ultimate confidence is in the Lord. As we depend more and more fully on him, he will give us the power to resist temptation.

What are some steps I can take to resist temptation?

Psalm 119:9 *How can a young person stay pure? By obeying your word and following its rules.*

God's word warns us against evil and shows us the way out of temptation.

1 Timothy 4:7-10 *Do not waste time arguing over godless ideas and old wives' tales. Spend your time and energy in training yourself for spiritual fitness. Physical exercise has some value, but spiritual exercise is much more important, for it promises a reward in both this life and the next. This is true, and everyone should accept it. We work hard and suffer much in order that people will believe the truth, for our hope is in the living God, who is the Savior of all people, and particularly of those who believe.*

The time to prepare for temptation is before it presses in upon us. If we prepare ourselves in the quiet times, we will have the spiritual wisdom, strength, and commitment to honor God in the face of intense desires and temptation.

1 Corinthians 10:13 *Remember that the temptations that come into your life are no different from what others experience. And God is faithful. He will keep the temptation from becoming so strong that you can't stand up against it. When you are tempted, he will show you a way out so that you will not give in to it.*
The Lord can lead us away from temptations. He can help us see the deception that blinds us. He can also help us anticipate the terrible consequences that will result from giving in to what we know is wrong. Instead of thinking that we have no chance of resisting, we can call on the Lord to lead us out of temptation.

What do I do when I fail?

1 John 1:9-2:2 *If we confess our sins to him, he is faithful and just to forgive us and to cleanse us from every wrong. If we claim we have not sinned, we are calling God a liar and showing that his word has no place in our hearts. My dear children, I am writing this to you so that you will not sin. But if you do sin, there is someone to plead for you before the Father. He is Jesus Christ, the one who pleases God completely. He is the sacrifice for our sins. He takes away not only our sins but the sins of all the world.*

God's grace is greater than our failure. His forgiveness overcomes our sin. Temptation only wins if it ultimately keeps us from turning back to God. No matter how often we fail, God welcomes us back through the love of Jesus Christ.

TIME

see also Stress

How can I best use time?

Psalm 90:12 *Teach us to make the most of our time, so that we may grow in wisdom.*

Ecclesiastes 3:1-11 *There is a time for everything, a season for every activity under heaven. A time to be born and a time to die. A time to plant and a time to harvest. A time to kill and a time to heal. A time to tear down and a time to rebuild. A time to cry and a time to laugh. A time to grieve and a time to dance. A time to scatter stones and a time to gather stones. A time to embrace and a time to turn away. A time to search and a time to lose. A time to keep and a time to throw away. A time to tear and a time to mend. A time to be quiet and a time to speak up. A time to love and a time to hate. A time for war and a time for peace. What do people really get for all their hard work? I have thought about this in connection with the various kinds of work God has given people to do. God has made everything beautiful for its own* time. He has planted eternity in the human heart, but even so, people cannot see the whole scope of God's work from beginning to end.

Valuing time begins with seeing it from God's perspective. When we do this, we learn that there is always time for accomplishing God's plans for our lives.

Ephesians 5:15-20 *Be careful how you live, not as fools but as those who are wise. Make the most of every opportunity for doing good in these evil days. Don't act thoughtlessly, but try to understand what the Lord wants you to do. Don't be drunk with wine, because that will ruin your life. Instead, let the Holy Spirit fill and control you. Then you will sing psalms and hymns and spiritual songs among yourselves, making music to the Lord in your hearts. And you will always give thanks for everything to God the Father in the name of our Lord Jesus Christ.*

Time is a gift. God gives us time so that we have the opportunity to serve him. When we give our time back to the Lord, he promises that it will not be wasted.

Revelation 1:3 *God blesses the one who reads this prophecy to the church, and he blesses all who listen to it and obey what it says. For the time is near when these things will happen.*

We live each day in the light of Christ's return. It inspires us to be faithful and gives us proper perspective on the fleeting nature of this earthly life.

How can I find the time I need?

Exodus 20:8-11 *Remember to observe the Sabbath day by keeping it holy. Six days a week are set apart for your daily duties and regular work, but the seventh day is a day of rest dedicated to the LORD your God. On that day no one in your household may do any kind of work. This includes you, your sons and daughters, your male and female servants, your livestock, and any foreigners living among you. For in six days the LORD made the heavens, the earth, the sea, and everything in them; then he rested on the seventh day. That is why the LORD blessed the Sabbath day and set it apart as holy.*

God designed us to rest one day out of seven. God's will for our lives includes time to worship and time to rest from our work.

TIMING OF GOD

see Will of God

TIRED

see also Renewal

Who can help me when I grow weary?

Psalm 68:35 *God is awesome in his sanctuary. The God of Israel gives power and strength to his people. Praise be to God!*

238

Psalm 145:14 *The LORD helps the fallen and lifts up those bent beneath their loads.*

Isaiah 40:29-31 *He gives power to those who are tired and worn out; he offers strength to the weak. Even youths will become exhausted, and young men will give up. But those who wait on the LORD will find new strength. They will fly high on wings like eagles. They will run and not grow weary. They will walk and not faint.*

Jeremiah 31:25 *I have given rest to the weary and joy to the sorrowing.*

The Lord is our source of rest and strength. When we come to him in praise, he refreshes our heart, mind, soul, and body. We release the burdens of life and draw strength from our Lord.

Ephesians 6:10 *Be strong with the Lord's mighty power.*

Habakkuk 3:19 *The Sovereign LORD is my strength! He will make me as surefooted as a deer and bring me safely over the mountains.*

Fatigue makes us more vulnerable to temptation and danger. When we are weary, we should turn to the Lord for rest and refreshment. In his power, we will be able to go into every situation with a clear head and a steady hand.

Hebrews 12:3, 12 *Think about all he endured when sinful people did such terrible things to him, so that you don't become weary and give up. . . . Take a new grip with your tired hands and stand firm on your shaky legs.*

When we are most tempted to give up, it helps to remind ourselves of the endurance of Jesus Christ. Though fully divine, Jesus was also fully human. He felt hungry, sad, and tired. He looked to his Father for strength and found the power for his every need. That same power is available to us if we seek it.

Does my weariness disappoint God?

Psalm 103:13-17 *The LORD is like a father to his children, tender and compassionate to those who fear him. For he understands how weak we are; he knows we are only dust. Our days on earth are like grass; like wildflowers, we bloom and die. The wind blows, and we are gone—as though we had never been here. But the love of the LORD remains forever with those who fear him. His salvation extends to the children's children.*

God made us flesh-and-blood human beings. He loves us as we are, even when we are too weary to do another thing. Like a tender parent who carries a sleeping child to bed, so the Lord cares for us when we are exhausted.

2 Corinthians 12:9 *Each time he said, "My gracious favor is all you need. My power works best in your weakness." So now I am glad to boast about my weaknesses, so that the power of Christ may work through me.*

Isaiah 41:10 *Don't be afraid, for I am with you. Do not be dismayed, for I am your God. I will strengthen you. I will help you. I will uphold you with my victorious right hand.*

Matthew 11:28 *Jesus said, "Come to me, all of you who are weary and carry heavy burdens, and I will give you rest."*

Our weariness often makes us more aware of God's faithfulness. In fact, some of our greatest joys come from watching God work when there's nothing else we can do.

TITHING

see also Giving, Money

How does tithing affect my own finances?

Malachi 3:8, 10 *"Should people cheat God? Yet you have cheated me! But you ask, 'What do you mean? When did we ever cheat you?' You have cheated me of the tithes and offerings due to me. . . . Bring all the tithes into the storehouse so there will be enough food in my Temple. If you do," says the LORD Almighty, "I will open the windows of heaven for you. I*

will pour out a blessing so great you won't have enough room to take it in! Try it! Let me prove it to you!"
God promises to meet our needs far and above our gifts to him. Tithing is God's means for supplying a variety of needs for his people. As we fulfill his command to meet others' needs, he graciously meets—and exceeds—our own.

Luke 6:38 *If you give, you will receive. Your gift will return to you in full measure, pressed down, shaken together to make room for more, and running over. Whatever measure you use in giving—large or small—it will be used to measure what is given back to you.*
If we give, God has promised to give to us more than we can imagine! Those who trust this promise find that they always have what they need when they need it.

WILL OF GOD

see also Guidance

Does God really have a plan for my life?

Psalm 139:3 *You chart the path ahead of me and tell me where to stop and rest. Every moment you know where I am.*

Psalm 32:8 *The LORD says, "I will guide you along the best pathway for your life. I will advise you and watch over you."*

Ephesians 1:11 *Because of Christ, we have received an inheritance from God, for he chose us from the beginning, and all things happen just as he decided long ago.*

Psalm 138:8 *The LORD will work out his plans for my life—for your faithful love, O LORD, endures forever. Don't abandon me, for you made me.*
God has a plan for our lives. It is not an unthinking, automated script that we must follow. It is a journey with various destinations and appointments and a great deal of freedom as to the pace and scope of the travel. God's plan for us will always have a sense of mystery, but we can be certain that he will guide us as long as we rely on his leading.

Jeremiah 29:11 *"I know the plans I have for you," says the LORD. "They are plans for good and not for disaster, to give you a future and a hope."*
Sometimes we are tempted to question God's will for our lives, thinking he has made a mistake. God promises to give us the best as we follow his ways. Ultimately, even what looks like a mistake can become the means to something wonderful.

How can I learn God's will for my life?

Romans 12:1-2 *Dear brothers and sisters, I plead with you to give your bodies to God. Let them be a living and holy sacrifice—the kind he will accept.*

When you think of what he has done for you, is this too much to ask? Don't copy the behavior and customs of this world, but let God transform you into a new person by changing the way you think. Then you will know what God wants you to do, and you will know how good and pleasing and perfect his will really is. Knowing God's will begins with knowing God. It also means giving ourselves fully to him. God holds nothing back from those who hold nothing back from him. As he transforms us into new people, we come to understand his ways and practice his purpose for our life.

Proverbs 3:6 *Seek his will in all you do, and he will direct your paths.*

1 John 5:14 *We can be confident that he will listen to us whenever we ask him for anything in line with his will.*
Prayer and the study of God's word are the most significant means that he uses to guide us.

WISDOM

What are the benefits of wisdom?

Proverbs 9:10 *Fear of the LORD is the beginning of wisdom. Knowledge of the Holy One results in understanding.*

Psalm 111:10 *Reverence for the LORD is the foundation of true wisdom. The rewards of wisdom come to all who obey him. Praise his name forever!* Wisdom is not simply knowing facts and figures; it is understanding that an all-powerful, all-knowing God has designed a moral universe with consequences for our good and evil choices. Wisdom begins with understanding our accountability to and our full dependence on our Creator. It's not what we know, but *who* we know.

Proverbs 3:21-26 *My child, don't lose sight of good planning and insight. Hang on to them, for they fill you with life and bring you honor and respect. They keep you safe on your way and keep your feet from stumbling. You can lie down without fear and enjoy pleasant dreams. You need not be afraid of disaster or the destruction that comes upon the wicked, for the LORD is your security. He will keep your foot from being caught in a trap.* Wisdom produces honor in our lives and protects us from trouble. Wise people know the difference between right and wrong and choose to do what's right. More than that, wisdom is choosing to apply God's truth and principles to our daily relationships and situations.

Proverbs 9:11-12 *Wisdom will multiply your days and add years to your life. If you become wise, you will be the one to benefit. If you scorn wisdom, you will be the one to suffer.*

Psalm 25:8-9 *The LORD is good and does what is right; he shows the proper path to those who go astray. He leads the humble in what is right, teaching them his way.*

Proverbs 3:5-6 *Trust in the LORD with all your heart; do not depend on your own understanding. Seek his will in all you do, and he will direct your paths.*

Proverbs 24:5 *A wise man is mightier than a strong man, and a man of knowledge is more powerful than a strong man.*
Wisdom will give us a richer, fuller life.

Matthew 7:24-27 *Anyone who listens to my teaching and obeys me is wise, like a person who builds a house on solid rock. Though the rain comes in torrents and the floodwaters rise and the winds beat against that house, it won't collapse, because it is built on rock. But anyone who hears my teaching and ignores it is foolish, like a person who builds a house on sand. When the rains and floods come and the winds beat against that house, it will fall with a mighty crash.*
Wisdom inspires confidence and prepares us for the most difficult times. Foolishness is a great risk and leaves us vulnerable to sure catastrophe.

How do we obtain wisdom?

1 John 2:27 *You have received the Holy Spirit, and he lives within you, so you don't need anyone to teach you what is true. For the Spirit teaches you all things, and what he teaches is true—it is not a lie. So continue in what he has taught you, and continue to live in Christ.*

1 Corinthians 2:15-16 *We who have the Spirit understand these things, but others can't understand us at all. How could they? For, "Who can know what the Lord is thinking? Who can give him counsel?" But we can understand these things, for we have the mind of Christ.*

Wisdom comes with the gift of the Holy Spirit. When we believe in Christ, we are given the mind of Christ.

James 1:5 *If you need wisdom—if you want to know what God wants you to do—ask him, and he will gladly tell you. He will not resent your asking.*
We need not be embarrassed to ask God for the wisdom and direction we need. He will certainly give it if we ask him.

Colossians 3:16 *Let the words of Christ, in all their richness, live in your hearts and make you wise. Use his words to teach and counsel each other. Sing psalms and hymns and spiritual songs to God with thankful hearts.*

Proverbs 1:5-7 *Let those who are wise listen to these proverbs and become even wiser. And let those who understand receive guidance by exploring the depth of meaning in these proverbs, parables, wise sayings, and riddles. Fear of the LORD is the beginning of knowledge. Only fools despise wisdom and discipline.*

Proverbs 1:23 *Come here and listen to me! I'll pour out the spirit of wisdom upon you and make you wise.*

Psalm 19:7 *The law of the LORD is perfect, reviving the soul. The decrees of the LORD are trustworthy, making wise the simple.*
God's word is our most reliable source of wisdom and insight. It speaks to all situations.

WITNESSING

How will God help me be a witness to my faith?

Mark 1:17 *Jesus called out to them, "Come, be my disciples, and I will show you how to fish for people!"*
Sharing our faith is a natural expression of our fellowship with Jesus. As we pray for sensitivity to his leading, he promises to direct us to those who are ready to hear the Good News of salvation.

Acts 1:8 *When the Holy Spirit has come upon you, you will receive power and will tell people about me everywhere—in Jerusalem, throughout Judea, in Samaria, and to the ends of the earth.*

Jesus gave us the Holy Spirit in order for us to be witnesses near and far—to our next-door neighbors and to the ends of the earth.

Acts 18:9-10 *One night the Lord spoke to Paul in a vision and told him, "Don't be afraid! Speak out! Don't be silent! For I am with you, and no one will harm you because many people here in this city belong to me."*
We are not alone when we witness. God is there to give us the words and the strength to proclaim his message.

But what if I find it difficult to share my faith?

Luke 12:8 *I assure you of this: If anyone acknowledges me publicly here on earth, I, the Son of Man, will openly acknowledge that person in the presence of God's angels.*

Daniel 12:3 *Those who are wise will shine as bright as the sky, and those who turn many to righteousness will shine like stars forever.*
Those who honor God by proclaiming the Good News of what he has done in Jesus Christ will be honored. There is no greater purpose in life than sharing the message that could make the eternal difference in someone's life.

2 Timothy 1:7-9 *God has not given us a spirit of fear and timidity, but of power, love, and self-discipline. So you must never be ashamed to tell others about our Lord. And don't be ashamed of me, either, even though I'm in prison for Christ. With the strength God gives you, be ready to suffer with me for the proclamation of the Good News. It is God who saved us and chose us to live a holy life. He did this not because we deserved it, but because that was his plan long before the world began—to show his love and kindness to us through Christ Jesus.*

When the enemy tries to intimidate us with lies about our inadequacies, we can call upon the promise that the truth will set us free to share our faith boldly.

WORK

How is my work important to the Lord?

1 Thessalonians 4:11-12 *This should be your ambition: to live a quiet life, minding your own business and working with your hands, just as we commanded you before. As a result, people who are not Christians will respect the way you live, and you will not need to depend on others to meet your financial needs.*

Work is God's plan for our lives. Those who work diligently experience many benefits in their own lives and bring benefits to others. God promises two basic rewards for faithful work: (1) having a more credible witness to nonbelievers and (2) having our needs met without having to financially depend on others.

Proverbs 13:11 *Wealth from get-rich-quick schemes quickly disappears; wealth from hard work grows.*
Honest, hard work is much better than get-rich-quick schemes. Money quickly gotten is often quickly wasted.

Romans 12:8 *If your gift is to encourage others, do it! If you have money, share it generously. If God has given you leadership ability, take the responsibility seriously. And if you have a gift for showing kindness to others, do it gladly.*
God blesses us when we do work that is in keeping with our gifts and abilities.

What does the Lord promise to those who work hard?

Proverbs 22:29 *Do you see any truly competent workers? They will serve kings rather than ordinary people.*
Faithful work makes a way for us to do greater work. God promises to bless us as we use the gifts he has given us.

Proverbs 10:4 *Lazy people are soon poor; hard workers get rich.*

Proverbs 21:5 *Good planning and hard work lead to prosperity, but hasty shortcuts lead to poverty.*

Colossians 3:23-24 *Work hard and cheerfully at whatever you do, as though you were working for the Lord rather than for people. Remember that the Lord will give you an inheritance as your reward, and the Master you are serving is Christ.*

God promises a reward to those who work hard. That reward can include—but is not limited to—financial prosperity. It may be the rewards of respect and personal satisfaction or the joy of contributing to the welfare of another.

How will God help me when my work is hard?

Psalm 145:14 *The LORD helps the fallen and lifts up those bent beneath their loads.*

As with any burden we bear, we can trust God to help us on the job.

WORRY

Where can I turn when worry overwhelms me?

Matthew 6:25-34 *So I tell you, don't worry about everyday life—whether you have enough food, drink, and clothes. Doesn't life consist of more than food and clothing? Look at the birds. They don't need to plant or*

252

harvest or put food in barns because your heavenly
Father feeds them. And you are far more valuable to
him than they are. Can all your worries add a single
moment to your life? Of course not. And why worry
about your clothes? Look at the lilies and how they
grow. They don't work or make their clothing, yet
Solomon in all his glory was not dressed as beautifully
as they are. And if God cares so wonderfully for flowers
that are here today and gone tomorrow, won't he more
surely care for you? You have so little faith! So don't
worry about having enough food or drink or clothing.
Why be like the pagans who are so deeply concerned
about these things? Your heavenly Father already
knows all your needs, and he will give you all you need
from day to day if you live for him and make the
Kingdom of God your primary concern. So don't worry
about tomorrow, for tomorrow will bring its own
worries. Today's trouble is enough for today.

The evidence of our heavenly Father's care is
everywhere, even in the most fleeting and
unnoticeable aspects of creation. God knows our
needs and promises to supply them. Worry
erodes our faith and robs us of the joy of
anticipating God's faithful provision.

What can I do with the problems that worry me?

Psalm 55:22 *Give your burdens to the LORD, and
he will take care of you. He will not permit the godly
to slip and fall.*

Philippians 4:6 *Don't worry about anything; instead, pray about everything. Tell God what you need, and thank him for all he has done.*

1 Peter 5:7 *Give all your worries and cares to God, for he cares about what happens to you.* Prayer and a godly perspective drive worry from our minds and hearts. Peace comes when we pray, release all our cares to the Lord, and focus our minds on the promises of God.

INDEX